<u>Dedication</u>

To all those I hired
And to those who hired me

Foreword

"Hiring Winners" is a winner. The information is presented in an economic, clear, and useful fashion all assisted by a marvelous sense of humor, and broad perspective. Yawar walks his talk, and it is obvious that he speaks from experience. In short he has been down this trail multiple times and learned more on every occasion.

In virtually all businesses, the cost of employees is the major cost. And yet it is surprising how often these major assets are acquired with little thought and less preparation. No one would purchase a critical piece of equipment without careful attention to the specifications, intended use, and life cycle costs of the same or similar equipment. And certainly the purchase of such equipment would not be left to a person or group possessing little or no technical expertise. And yet when it comes to new employees the process and procedures of good employment practice seem to fall by the way side, if indeed they were ever on the road. Strange!

The costs for such neglect can be staggering, and they only begin with the wages and benefits lost when a poorly chosen employee has to be terminated. Opportunities lost, negative environments created, deadlines missed, customers disappointed and disappeared. And there is a different way! Choosing winners is doubtless an art, but it is an art founded on a substantial skill base. Yawar provides us with a clear, and I would say brilliant, introduction to that skill base. And best of all he points the way to the realms of High Art. It isn't perfect, and it won't always work, but this book will certainly enhance the odds. And as we all know, in the competitive business environment, every little bit helps. And what Yawar provides is definitely more than a "little bit."

Harrison Owen

Author of Open Space Technology

7808 River Falls Drive

Potomac, Maryland 20845

Why this book?

"There's something rare, something finer far, something much more scarce than ability; it's the ability to recognize ability."

In my practice of helping business leaders develop a winning culture, the thing that I have been most keenly aware of, is the need to hire winners. It is true that good training can achieve much. But it is equally true that no matter how good the training course or the trainer there are some things which can't be 'trained in'. Losers will never become winners because of training. As they say, 'If you want someone to climb trees, hire a monkey.' Hiring a rabbit and training him will get you nowhere because there are certain intrinsic abilities, orientations and attitudes that are required even for the training to take hold. The qualities, characteristics, behaviors, values and beliefs that make a winner must necessarily be hired. Skills can be trained. You can train a person of high integrity how to write accurate financial accounts. But to try to inculcate integrity into someone who is essentially dishonest is not something that any amount of training can achieve.

How can we find out what these intrinsic qualities are? How can we ensure that the person we hire comes pre-loaded with these qualities and that he or she has and will continue to exercise them? How can I know what the effect was of their displaying and practicing the desirable behaviors in their life in the past, so that I have some idea of what I am likely to see here? How do the values and motivations of the individual sync with my organization's culture and ideology? What is the cost of all this? All these and other questions and their answers, is what this book is about.

Effective interviewing is the best and perhaps the only way to ensure that you identify what a person is truly capable of, their strengths, orientation, what makes them tick and what they have proven that they can do.

The basic premise is, 'What they did well before, they can do again.'

While being all for experimentation, hiring is not a place that I recommend it. Many people during the interview will tell you about all that they dream to do. While I am listening to them, all I am hearing is, 'He did not do this ever before. So he is going to learn at my expense.' I am not saying that you should not invest in this kind of thing. I am saying that you should do that consciously and not be suddenly surprised to see what all your new hire has to learn before he can become productive. You may well ask, 'What are these qualities? What is the best way to identify and ensure that the person I am hiring has them? Are there any tools to help me in achieving this goal?' Can I assess all this in a 10 minute interview? Is there some formula?

Of formulae & psychometrics

One word of caution; for the desperate there are many out there who offer to custom design psychometric instruments which they claim will 'find' for you the exact type of person you need. They tell you that all you need to do is to tell them the qualities that you are looking for and that they will then design a questionnaire which will show you faultlessly if the individual has those qualities or not. They tell you that this is a foolproof way to hire the right people. They ask you for a hefty fee for this service. They lie through their teeth.

They don't tell you that any psychometric test is only as good as the honesty and frankness with which it is answered. And they don't tell you (and indeed why should they when it is so obviously visible) that no matter what you say to a candidate who has come for an interview, he wants to be hired and will consciously or unconsciously answer the questionnaire in a way that he believes will show him in the best light. The result? Garbage in, garbage out. Also they don't tell you that psychometric testing for hiring is illegal in the US and several other countries and will open you to expensive litigation. So please avoid all psychometric questionnaires like the plague when it comes to hiring. Psychometric testing is fine in developmental situations, when you are looking to train people and help them to assess themselves. There is less or no tension in such situations and the results of the test are far more reliable. An Assessment Center on the other hand is an excellent tool that can supplement the hiring process but it needs expert design and facilitation to give you the results you need. But it is a good tool.

Our course, **'Hiring Winners'** is a two day module that is designed to help people understand themselves and to teach them how to use the skills of probing, asking good questions and effective listening to ensure that they are able to verify that the interviewee actually has the attitudes and skills that you need to hire. This book is the essence of what I have learned in teaching and practice of this technique over more than 26 years. This book is about doing. It teaches the tools and shows you how you can hire winners most effectively.

I hope you enjoy reading this book and would encourage you to practice what you read. Knowledge is only as good as its practice. I have deliberately kept the writing simple and oriented towards practice. The 'he' includes 'she' and 'she' includes 'he'. This is intended to be a manual for practicing Managers and not a book of theory for students. Please do mail me at yawarbaig@gmail.com I would love to hear from you.

Who is a Winner?

I believe that before we actually talk about the mechanics of how to hire winners, it will be useful to ask ourselves, "Who is a winner?"

I want to share with you my own definition of a winner.

You are a winner if you are willing to take responsibility. To take ownership for all that you say and do. For the effect of your words and actions on others and on the world. Not merely to accept accountability but to actively seek it. To stand up and say, "Here I am. You can count on me." And if things go wrong, as sometimes they will, to say, "I am responsible for what has happened. Here is what I learnt from this. And this is how we will ensure this never happens again."

We all start in the same place. We all start as idealists. I have yet to see a child who was not an idealist. We all want to make a difference to the world we live in, to do great things and to be remembered. We all want to be winners. But how many people actually achieve that? And why not?

Let's see what happens and why.

We all start as Idealists. Then life happens. Things happen where people let you down. Often the very people who you counted on to support you. People deceive and lie and cheat and sacrifice long term benefits for short term gains. They are corrupt and this and that and the other. So as all these things happen, we get onto the slide and start sliding downwards.

From being **Idealists**, we become **Optimists** (because idealism is tough to put down, especially when you are young and energetic) and then we become **Realists**, then **Pessimists**. Along the way we acquire 'advisors'; people who take us aside and 'talk some sense' into us. They tell us, "Look, don't be a fool. Get real. This is the real world. Be practical. Be realistic. Ideals are okay to talk about. They don't work and will get you into trouble. Forget all this. Look around you. How many people do you see actually working for 'ideals'?"

You will say, "But look at what Yawar is saying!! What about that?"

Your advisor will say, "Let him talk. What does it matter? That is his job. He is a teacher and trainer. Let him talk. You eat the nice snacks, meet your friends, have a nice time and go home. Forget him."

And slowly we also become like our 'advisors'. We become **Cynics**.

From Idealist to Optimist to Realist to Pessimist to Cynic; on the slide.

Cynics are also very popular at parties as they are witty and make cynical remarks and make people laugh. But cynicism is a cancer. It eats the soul from inside. But unlike cancer, it is contagious and spreads. Cynics can be intimidating and will inhibit many people with enthusiasm by making fun of them. Then good words like, integrity, service and compassion become the butt of jokes. Lethal.

And in the end, at the bottom of the pile, we become **Indifferent**. We stop caring what happens. That is the real bottom of the pit.

You know why people get angry and fight you when you say idealistic things? Because we remind them of what they were like one day. The flame of idealism is possible to dampen. But it is impossible to kill. It will remain alive as long as we live. It dies when we die. It is what we do with our life experiences that affects our idealism. We often have little or no choice over what happens to us, but we have total freedom to react to it in any way we like. It is like a mathematical equation: its two sides produce the result. One side is given to us and the other side is left to us to write whatever number we like.

But the result depends on the whole equation, not on any one side alone. If we remember this and ensure that we write what needs to be written to get the result we need, then it doesn't matter what the equation comes written with.

We will still have a positive result. If on the other hand we get overwhelmed with the number the equation came with and either not write our own number or do it without thinking then the result can be negative.

Let me illustrate with a real-life example how by consciously choosing to respond instead of merely reacting you can convert a potentially negative situation into a positive one.

I was the Manager of New Ambadi Estate in South India and we were facing a tough union situation. It was essential for us that the government in the person of its representatives in the Department of Labor were on our side, so to speak, because any case would go up before the Commissioner of Labor for conciliation.

What happened was as follows: One day the Labor Officer came to see me. In the course of conversation he asked for a donation to the Labor Sports Fund as the Department of Labor was organizing an Annual Sports Day. I agreed and asked my Head Clerk to give him the amount he wanted. After some more small talk he left. Some weeks passed and our conflict with the union on the estate was coming to a head.

So I decided that I would go and meet the Labor Officer and apprise him of the situation in case of the labor unrest that we were anticipating.

When I reached his office and sent in my card his peon told me, "He is asking you to wait." This was a bit of a departure from the normal courtesy that was extended every time I went to see him when he would immediately call me or ask me to sit in an anteroom. In this case I was asked to sit in the usual waiting room which was very sparsely furnished with hardly a decent chair to sit on. I kept standing. After about 20 minutes when I had just about decided to leave without seeing him, he called me in. As soon as I entered the door of his office, he started shouting, "You people only think of us when you need us, eh! When we need your help you promise help and do nothing. Why should I help you when you need me? I will show you what we can do....." He went on in this vein for almost 5 minutes. To say that I was shocked was to put it mildly. I did not know what hit me. I could literally feel myself grow hot and cold inside. I felt insulted and very angry. But consciously I did not show any of this on my face. I simply stood and listened to him in silence. At last he stopped and said, "Please have a seat."

I looked at him and said, "No Sir I think I will go now. I will come back later when you have cooled down. Then we can talk. Excuse me." I turned to go. He called out and said, "No Sir. Please sit down. I will talk to you." So I sat down. Then I asked him, "Tell me what was all this about? Why are you so angry?" He now looked down and said, "You promised that you would give a donation to our Sports Fund and then you gave the money to the Factories Officer so that he could make his quota while I was the one who asked you for the amount."

I said, "Can I please use your phone to call my office to find out what happened? I have no idea what you are talking about." I called my office and learnt that the donation could not be given the day he had come to see me, so he left saying that he would send someone the next day to collect the cash once we had drawn it from the bank. The next day the Factories Officer came and asked for the donation and my Head Clerk gave the amount to him thinking that he had been sent by the Labor Officer. Little did he know that the two of them had individual quotas and that the Labor Officer had not sent the Factories Officer at all.

Once I had all the details, I explained the situation to him and he realized that he had flown off his handle without cause. He became very apologetic and ashamed of his own behavior and apologized. All that remained for me to win the day was to be magnanimous and accept his apology which I did.

The result was that he became extremely cooperative in everything in order to make up for his behavior and was a great help to us in the crisis of the lockout. All because I did not react to his anger with anger. I can't say that I controlled my own anger that day as a result of a thought out strategy. I think I just got lucky. But I learnt the lesson nevertheless. Emotions that you name, you control. Those you can't or won't name, control you.

There is always your side of the equation that is in your control. Think and write the correct number and you will win.

Idealism
is
impossible
to kill.

When people allow themselves to live lives that result in many negative experiences they tend to become cynical. When people who have allowed themselves to become cynical and indifferent, meet you, who are an idealist, they are reminded of what they were like one day. And they hate what they see in your eyes; they hate what they have chosen to do to themselves. They believe that if they can make you shut up, then somehow all will be well. Because they are one of the many who believe this fallacy, that if one can make someone who speaks the truth to shut up; then one can remain comfortable in one's falsehood. They refuse to face the reality that the truth is the truth even if no one speaks it.

The thing to do therefore, if you want to be a winner is to light the lamps of other's idealism. And the only way to do that is to ensure that your own lamp never goes out. The way to do that is never to lower your ideals in the name of expedience, or diplomacy. By all means use your wisdom and skill in putting across your ideals in as convincing and acceptable a way as you can, but never lower the standard. For the standard is our only protection against the slide into mediocrity and oblivion.

Remember that no person or nation lives forever. But their thoughts, their goals, their ideals and what they stood for endures long after they have become dust. That is what we stand for; ideals that have stood the test of time and which we carry forward to generations who will come, long after we have gone.

Winners are people who instinctively understand these things, even if they may not be able to state them clearly. You can see this from the choices that they have made in life. Choices that the method you will learn in this book will help you to see. Look for them and recognize them. And remember that the truest way to recognize them is sometimes to recognize the fear and humility that you will sense in your own soul as you listen to someone else's story.

Winners are people who challenge the status quo. Who refuse to accept the 'accepted' just because those around them accept it. Winners are people who will challenge you to live by your stated ideals. Who refuse to pretend that they still respect you if you give in to your fears and lie to yourself. Winners by the look in their eyes remind you that you have failed yourself, and by their look give you the courage to get up and start again. Winners disagree with you and challenge you to prove your theories. They make you exercise more rigor in what you do, refuse to accept mediocrity, set goals that frighten you so that the adrenaline you need to accomplish them is poured into your veins. Winners challenge you to constantly learn, grow and mature. They challenge you to prove to them and to yourself that you are indeed worthy of respect.

Of course this is not all about hiring alone. It is even more about training and grooming and developing people. However the point I want to make is that hiring the right person is critical in making all the rest of it effective. If the person does not have the capacity or has the wrong sort of attitude, then training does not achieve the desired result and leaves you frustrated.

Key Qualities of Winners

In more than 26 years of teaching leadership to people from multiple nationalities, cultures, religions, genders and races on 3 continents, I believe I've learned some important lessons on what makes one a 'Winner'. Winners are leaders and so I have used the two words interchangeably.

I asked myself this question: 'What qualities are essential for winning/leading?' Not what is nice to have, useful, beneficial and so on, but what is essential. My definition of 'essential' is, 'something without which it can't be done.'

One last line: All this stuff will seem simple and it is. The trick is in implementing.

The rules are the same for everyone. They are:

Rule # 1:   **Excuses don't change facts**
Rule # 2:   **If in doubt refer to Rule # 1.**

There are 7 – essentials for 'Winning'

1. **Vision**
2. **Inspire followers**
3. **Single-mindedness of purpose**
4. **Strategy**
5. **Faith**
6. **Deal with Ambiguity**
7. **Execution**

Needless to say as you practice them you will and must add to this understanding and share it with others, including myself.

People often ask me for the secret of leadership. I tell them to come close and then I whisper it in their ears; after all it is a secret, see? It is one word; DISCIPLINE.
That is all. Every one of us has the same time; 24 hours. It is what we do in it that counts. It is not the amount of our resources but what we did with them. It is not the

 talents that we were born with but how we leveraged them and used them which will determine how they benefit us.

1. Vision
In the beginning is the Vision.

Naturally, if we want to go somewhere, we need to be clear about two things:

1. Where is that 'somewhere'?

2. What is it that is so compelling and attractive about it?

The more clearly we are able to visualize the benefits of achieving the vision, the more staying power we will have to achieve it. The reality of all things worthy of striving for is that a lot of that striving will have to be done, unsung, in the dark of the night when our energy and inspiration is at the lowest ebb. It is at these times when we need the glow of the benefits of achieving the vision, shining uncompromised on the horizon so that we can ignore the pain and discouragement and continue to put one step ahead of the next.

Inspiration to me is not something that comes like a bolt out of the blue and takes the unsuspecting soul unawares. Inspiration is often the result of a great deal of dissatisfaction with the current state that leads to honest questioning about the purpose of life and deep reflection and a sustained inner struggle with the real issues that one faces in one's life. This is sometimes very painful and never easy to do. But when one stays with the questions long enough, the answers start to appear.

These answers again are not in the form of clear cut road maps but more like a hazy sign, on a dark and misty night, seen at the very edge of the limit of your headlights. You can just about make out the direction it is pointing in. All the rest is up to you and your ingenuity. And it does not tell you anything about the difficulties of the path. One common factor that you can rely on is the fact that there will be difficulties. That is something that I believe the potential leader can bet on.

The trick is to understand what to do with the difficulty when you are faced with it. The common tendency is to moan and groan and say, "Why me?" Not so common is to be happy to face the difficulty since you believe it indicates the promise of reward, once you can surmount it.

The truth is that in life rewards have to be earned and that happens by overcoming challenges. So every time you stand up and say, 'I want to gain something', a challenge stands up to face you. Then if you overcome the challenge you gain the reward. Another way to understand this is to think of surfing – the higher you want to go, the bigger the wave that you have to ride. Yes, you can go under, but that is the spice of it. That is what gives it the taste.

We don't choose our 'purpose' in life. We discover it. When we find it, then our life enters a state of grace. It is like the difference between a fish in water and outside it. Out of water, a fish is a clumsy creature, gasping for breath and flopping on the sand. When you throw it into the river, it vanishes in a flash; the epitome of beauty, grace and speed. Same fish; different worlds. It is the same with us. If we are in a role that is not in sync with our purpose, we find it hard going, energy sapping and a drag all around. But when we are doing something that ignites the heart, we have boundless energy, ideas flash like lightning and we energize everyone else around us.

A method that I use is to ask what this difficulty has been sent to teach me. This comes from my belief that nothing happens by accident and that all of life is a prepared plan that is unfolding and that I am the one who has the exciting task of walking the path as it appears before me. So every difficulty comes with a fortune cookie inside that tells you what the lesson is, provided you can get to it. Blaming others for creating the difficulty or carping about it only indicates that you are not ready to become a real leader yet.

When we question the purpose of the difficulty and ask, 'What can I learn from this?' we find that our perspective takes on a whole new meaning. We are no longer grounded in the negativity of blaming and feeling sorry for ourselves but are freed to look for creative and new ways of overcoming the difficulty. The enormity of the task itself becomes the biggest motivator, as one is conscious only of the prospect of great reward. The fact that this is not easy then becomes easy to accept and understand, and one even says, "If it was easy, I

 wouldn't want it. It would not make the victory so sweet!'

Interestingly, the route to the state of grace is through great effort. It is a path that is difficult and strewn with the wrecks of those that went before. It is easy to see this in physical examples of martial arts, sports and other physical-skill related things. The reality is that it is the same path in challenges of the mind and of the spirit. And very often, in the latter events the route is even more difficult, for the goal is in the wining of people's hearts and the change is in their minds.

I have reflected very often on why it is more difficult in the non-physical endeavors. My understanding is that it is because of the paradox that in the physical effort it is very often impossible or very difficult to give up once you have gone beyond the halfway point, often called the 'point of no return'. Take mountaineering as an example. Once you have made the effort to reach halfway, it is easier and shorter to go on no matter how difficult it looks, than to turn around and return.

What aids this is the fact that the path is not entirely unknown and you know it has an end and you know where that is.

In the journey of the spirit, the path is unknown, the duration of the effort needed is unknown and it is extremely easy to give up. There is no point of no return. You can give up and get back to your original state in an instant. That carrot is always hanging in front of the nose. And to make matters worse, the pain and suffering of confusion and emotional turmoil, which is often worse than the physical pain, is unseen and uncelebrated by others, who in a physical challenge, often provide the necessary impetus by cheering from the sidelines. And when you give up the spiritual and emotional struggle, there is no fear of shame and ridicule by others, since nobody knew you were in there anyway.

That is the reason why most people shy away from accepting challenges of the mind and spirit, even though they may know in their hearts that those are the true challenges that have the capacity to change their destiny. It requires a strong internal focus, a real desire to make a mark in life, no desire for approval from others, and a willingness to stay with the task irrespective of the time it takes or the apparent lack of 'progress'.

It is a path that challenges all previously held beliefs and that is full of the fear of the unknown. It is a path that tests one with the challenge of living the life that one previously only talked about. It challenges us to not only put our money where our mouth is but to demonstrate commitment by taking the leap of faith into the new way of life with no guarantees of safety nets. But the good news is that history is full of examples of those that accepted this challenge and succeeded.

It is important to remember that the wrecks on the path of leadership are of those who gave up midway. Those that persevered, are the ones that went through and whose leadership often lives on long after they themselves passed on into history.

What seems to be critical in this struggle and something that gives sustenance when one is moving through an arid waste is the enormity of the goal. No heroic effort was ever made for a minor goal. Enormous goals call for enormous effort and have in them the capacity to keep the motivation alive in the face of all odds.

I believe that this is in the very nature of the goal. If you find your dedication flagging midway, look at your goal and ask yourself, "Is this goal worthy of my effort?" Aim for a larger goal and you will find that the wellsprings of your energy once again start to flow.

No vision worth the name is possible to achieve alone.

 So one needs others. And that is where the catch is. How do we make others dream our dream? And not only dream it but feel it, be inspired by it, own it and make it their own such that they will now work to make it come true? How can we do all this and do it as fast as possible?

2. Inspire followers

How can I make you dream my dream?

My dream is in my heart. How do I transfer it into your heart and that too in such a way that it fires up your imagination as it fires up mine? It is not about 'explaining'.

Have you ever tried to explain some very powerful and sublime lines of poetry, especially in another language? You will realize what I mean.

Many times, explanations kill the spirit of the dream. Yet what choice do we have but to explain? So explain we must – but in a way that retains the spirit.

How?

By total and complete, even irrational, belief in the dream. Why is this total belief and passion required? Because passion drives behavior and behavior drives results. If there is no passion the behavior necessary to achieve the dream will not appear. Passion can be seen and heard in your voice. Passion speaks louder than words. And only passion convinces; not words. The finest words coming out of the mouth of someone who doesn't really believe in them, fall flat.

Broken sentences, bad grammar, even a loss of words, goes straight to the heart if what is in the heart can be seen. All sorts of studies on non-verbal communication support this. It is what is in the eyes, what the body says and what the tone of your voice conveys that convinces far more than the words themselves.

That is not to say that one does not need words. But that words only support the message. They don't convey the message. Now that may sound strange to you to hear me say that words don't convey the message. But I am convinced as a result of speaking to literally a couple of hundred thousand people in my life – that hearts speak to hearts. The words are the same. In one case, they penetrate. In another they fall on deaf ears. And that has to do with the speech of the hearts.

So our own belief in our dream and our own conviction about what will be accomplished and how critical, essential, beneficial, enriching, empowering or whatever the benefits of realizing the dream are; that is what will penetrate to the hearts of the listeners. Inspiring is not only about making speeches but even more about demonstrating commitment.

The only rule to remember is:

People listen with their eyes.

Credibility is the single biggest asset of the leader. If a leader loses credibility he/she is finished; more so because not only is credibility very difficult to regain but in most circumstances it is impossible to regain with the same set of people or in the same place. The thing which reinforces or destroys credibility most is when the leader does not follow his/her own rules. When there is a gap between your talk and your walk, credibility falls through it and disappears. People don't care what you say; they look to see what you do. This is the reason why the courage to lead from the front is critical. A leader who makes an exception for himself loses respect.

The best way to not only demonstrate your own sense of responsibility and courage as well as to reinforce the message that there are no exceptions is to create a clear system of accountability and to follow it. The metrics must then be adhered to scrupulously. I have not used the word, 'enforced' because I believe that with good leadership the need to 'enforce' becomes progressively less. Not to say that you should not enforce if there is a need to. Indeed you must and make an example of it as well. But if you as the leader are the person who is most adherent to the ethics and values then enforcing these on others will not be necessary. People will develop a culture of self-accountability and will govern themselves. It is then only necessary to watch it happen. The leader must epitomize the vision. There are no exceptions to this. When followers think of the vision, it is the face of the leader that they must see before them. Leadership is a contact sport. It is about getting out there in the field, fighting where it is thickest, falling down and getting up every time but never giving up. This is not about using a losing strategy over and over. It is about staying true to the vision but changing strategy and tactics as the situation and challenges demand. Flexibility, openness and the willingness to change are huge assets and very critical to success. However the goal, the standard of excellence, the bar must never be compromised.

If you settle for anything but the best, then you have betrayed the vision. And that, is death.

Compassion

Finally but not lastly is the importance of taking care of followers. They used to say, 'An army marches on its belly.' This refers not only to managing supply chains but to the whole philosophy of leadership. Bonding between the leader and follower is a matter of the heart. And that happens when the follower feels taken care of, over and beyond the call of duty. Just as the follower gets a medal for doing more than his due, so also the leader gets an emotional medal translating to faithfulness when he/she demonstrates concern and compassion for their people.

There is the story of the woman, a single parent at the checkout desk in a store on Christmas Eve; very sad because she did not have time to buy a baseball glove for her 5 year old. As the store closes and she is about to leave, the manager walks up and gives her a gift. Guess what it was. The issue is not about what it costs. It is about the thoughtfulness, the understanding, the concern and the compassion for the team member that the action demonstrates. When people feel understood and they have confidence that their leader is in their corner, then they are willing to push the boundaries and do more than merely what is expected.

I call this the 'Critical Moment'. The leader must live with awareness; must be observant and sensitive to people and atmosphere. Critical Moments are incidents that have the potential to create great influence on the minds of many more than those involved in the incident itself. Critical Moments can't be created by the leader but they can be leveraged when they occur provided the leader is aware of them.

I remember an incident – one of many such – that happened to me which illustrates my Critical Moment theory rather well. It happened when I used to work in the tea gardens in South India. One day just before coming home for lunch I went to Iyerpadi Hospital as I had a headache and needed some medicine. When I reached there I found the staff in a frenzy running here and there. I caught hold of one of them and asked her what the matter was. She said, "We have a woman in labor and she is extremely anemic. She needs a blood transfusion immediately or she and the baby will die."

"So why are you all in such a tizzy?" I asked.

"We are looking for her relatives (Dalits) to donate blood", she said. "But they are all in the field and we can't get hold of any of them."

"Take my blood", I said. "I am O+ and have blood that looks like lube oil; it is so rich in hemoglobin. So take what you need."

The nurse looked at me in shock. "You will donate your blood for this woman?" she asked me in surprise. Her surprise was because the woman was a poor Dalit and I am not. So how could I be agreeing to have my blood flowing in her and her child's veins? This was unimaginable for her given the local social system that she was also a product of. She looked at me in astonishment and disbelief, quite prepared if I had done a retake and withdrawn my offer. However I didn't.

I told her to get on with it and take my blood. But she still would not move, almost rooted to her place, simply looking at me as if I was speaking a language that she could not understand.

While we were talking, the RMO Dr. John Philip (a wonderful physician and good friend) came along and asked me what was happening. I told him the story and he said to the nurse, "He wants to give his blood. What is your problem? Just take it or the woman will die." That broke the spell and in short order I was laid down and bled. Two bottles of blood were taken and I was then given a cup of coffee and sent home. No idea what happened to my headache. Maybe donating blood is a cure for headache.

I went home, had lunch and my afternoon nap; a very civilized activity that I had to give up when I left the plantations. When I woke up to go to the office, my butler Bastian came to me and said, "Master, Golden Mountain (literal translation of the name of the man, which was Thangamalai – Bastian used to do these things sometimes) is here to see you with the whole Works Committee."

At that time there were some rumblings going on about the annual bonus which was to be paid in 2 months and so I immediately thought that perhaps it was some agitation on that account that the Works Committee had come to tell me about. I was a little irritated as well because I didn't encourage the union leaders to meet me at home as I liked to keep official and personal business separate. A very sound policy at all times.

When I went out to the front of the bungalow, I saw the whole Works Committee, all 24 of them lined up behind Thangamalai. They greeted me in the usual way by making namaskaar, "Namaskaaram Dorai," Thangamali said on behalf of all of them. I returned the greeting, "Namaskaaram. What can I do for you?"

Wordlessly, Thangamalai came up to me and before I realized what he was doing, bent down and touched my feet in reverence. And behind him all the others started to do the same, one by one. I stepped back in amazement. "What on earth is this for? Don't do this. You know I don't like people touching my feet and bowing before me."

"Dorai, today you have to let us do this. Don't stop us today", said Thangamalai. "Why are you doing this?" I was still upset with them. "What has happened?"

"Dorai, today you did something that has never been done before in the history of these hills. You gave your blood to one of us."

"So what's the big deal? Wouldn't you have done it for me, if I was in need of blood?"

"Dorai, we have always given our blood and even our lives for the managers of these plantations. But your people never do it for us. You are the first of them who has ever done this for one of us. So we bow to you with love and respect. You are our Kadavul (term of high respect which literally means god in Tamil)."

"I am not anyone's god. I am a human being like you and I did what I consider my duty. How are the mother and child?"

"They are both well Dorai and they owe their lives to you."

The point here is that I could not have made this incident happen even if I had wanted to. But the fact that I was fortunate enough to be in the right place and then had acted according to my principles paid great dividends in enhancing my credibility and was very useful during some very stressful times that were to come later that year.

Compassion is essential for the leader to have. Feeling the pain of someone enables you to take the right decision. This does not mean that compassionate people can't take hard decisions. It just means that they will take it ways that don't increase the hurt or add anger to it. And it means that they will do what is necessary to mitigate the hardship of the change.

3. Single-mindedness of purpose
Never compromise the standard

I have found that as you embark on your vision, if the vision is difficult, then there is pressure to settle for less. People give you examples of others who are doing more or less similar things and are 'successful'. They will ask you, 'Why do we need all this?' 'Why can't we do it with less?'

The answer is, 'Because of the value of differentiation.'

Differentiation creates Brand
Brand creates Loyalty
Loyalty creates Influence

Without differentiation you are 'a grain of rice in a sack'. It is essential never to lose this focus. Never to allow anyone to compromise the standard. Never to settle for less. For we will be remembered by our legacy. So the legacy must never be compromised.

What will help to keep on track is clarity about the vision and its benefits which make it unique. This is the reason that in my view the 'vision' that many companies articulate about becoming a 'billion dollar business by year so-and-so' is not very energizing. After all how charged up can you get about selling more widgets?

Money is an important consideration in terms of returns but money does not motivate. Increasing turnover is not the reason for which your people will 'want to come to work'. It is not the reason that people will dream to join your organization. It is not the thing that they will speak proudly about to their peers and in their groups nor the reason why they will defend you and your vision or root for your success. Money is what they buy bread with. Not what they will be willing to sacrifice their best for. People must be clear how they are unique. Money is the lowest common denominator for all business. It is not anything unique, no matter how much of it is there. So do give some thought to what makes you unique. Without uniqueness there is no differentiation. Without differentiation you are a grain of rice in a sack. There is loyalty for brand and brand is the other name for differentiation. Be it product, service, company of individual, for success to happen brand must be built. Profit is the result of brand and not vice versa.

Strategy

How will you get to where you want to be?

Having a vision and being able to convey it successfully to the Core Group leads us to the next challenge i.e. what is the way to achieve this vision?

This is a very big challenge for many visionaries and many succeed because they have had the good fortune or  the foresight to have someone in their Core Group who can do the math, draw the lines and create an actual road map. The 'visionary' temperament is often very impatient with detail. But as they say, 'God is in the details.' Without the details, the vision will remain a dream, to energize people for a while and then to disappear; perhaps even to be lodged in the back of the mind somewhere in a box labeled, 'IF ONLY' but never to see the light of day. It is strategy that must be built; a good honest simple, robust strategy that will lead to the achievement of the vision.

Let us look at the elements of strategy to see what makes it good. There are three requirements that any strategy must fulfill if it is to be successful.

1. Simple to understand
2. Simple to implement
3. In your control

Simple to Understand

There is a difference between being 'simple' and being 'simplistic'. If you are one of those who likes to devise complicated methods that need your personal intervention to work and this makes you feel indispensable then you are looking at a model which will at best grace some research thesis on all those strategies that did not work.

Gandhiji's strategy of civil disobedience was simple but by no means simplistic. It was easy for anyone to understand, had a clear target, stood on admirable universally accepted principles of truthfulness, honesty, integrity and non-violence. Nobody can argue against any of them. Yet it was these same principles which shook the foundation of the mighty British Empire and eventually gave India its freedom.

Simple to Implement

This is the second most important principle in a good strategy; it must be simple to implement. Not everyone who will work with you will be as educated, intelligent, handsome, sexy or brilliant as you are. So creating complex models on fancy computer programs and making dazzling presentations as part of the implementation process will fail.

The Bombay Dabbawalas are a classic case of a simple to implement strategy creating a business that does not merely conform to global standards but sets a new benchmark for global quality and delivery standards. It is run by, for the most part illiterate, village folk and has no MBAs or computers in sight. Maybe that is a reason for its success. Many times I have seen people taking refuge behind smokescreens of feasibility reports, financial scenarios, and breakeven analyses and in the process, forget to do business; to hit the street and sell. That unfortunately is the only economic activity.

In your control

In my view this is one of the most important touchstones for any strategy to succeed. Is it in your control?

Once upon a time there was a sparrow which had built a nest in a corn field. As the corn grew, so did her chicks until they were now learning to fly. One day when the sparrow returned from work to the nest in the evening, her chicks were very worried and said to her, 'Mom, the farmer and his sons were here and they said that they are going to cut the corn tomorrow. What will happen to us?'

'Tell me exactly what you heard,' said the sparrow.

'Well, the farmer said to his sons, 'Go to the village council tomorrow and tell them that we need help to cut our field so can they please announce this so that our neighbors will come to help us. We can start cutting in the morning.'

'Don't worry,' said the sparrow. 'Nothing will happen. Meanwhile you keep doing your flying lessons.'

Nothing happened for the next few days. Then one day the chicks reported, 'Mom, the farmer came today with his sons and said, 'None of the neighbors have turned up. The field is now ready to be cut. Go to your uncles and tell them to come tomorrow. We will cut the corn.' The sparrow said, 'Don't worry, nothing will happen. Keep flying.' Two days later, the chicks reported, 'Mom, today the farmer came and said to his sons, 'Your uncles also did not come. Tomorrow morning we will start cutting the corn ourselves.' The sparrow said, 'Okay kiddos, time to go.'

I have seen many excellent strategies which depend on government ordinances, community support, social change and so on in order to succeed. They all fail. On the other hand we have the excellent example of the many women's self help groups in the field of education, microcredit and so forth which are huge success stories. The golden rule in strategy is, **'If it is not in your control, it is not in your control.'**

In that case you will need to redefine it and take responsibility for it to make it work.

One way is to create a pilot project which may gain for you the initial interest to convince others to back it.

Measuring with merciless accuracy

The difference between a brilliant strategy and one that is merely good is measurement. Metrics don't make a bad strategy good but they make a good one brilliant. Metrics don't necessarily correct faults but they show up faults before they become catastrophes. Metrics catch mistakes early so that they can be corrected. Metrics catch good ideas early so that even more importantly they can be rewarded. The key in good metrics is not only to measure but to be clear about what to measure. This requires a thorough knowledge of the subject to know what a certain measurement is telling us. Time spent during the planning stage in creating good metrics is time very well spent. Needless to state, no metric is good for all time or even necessary. So metrics must be continually examined, revised and changed to keep them useful.

Metrics measure progress in all sorts of ways; speed, use of resources, waste, or satisfaction. Metrics tell us not only how we are doing but also how that measures up against global standards. Metrics help us to put things in perspective. Metrics are not a way of policing. Metrics are meant to help us to be fair, objective and responsive to the contributor, customer and ourselves. Metrics help us to establish the value and worth of what we are doing. They help us to prove that we are fair and just. They help us to prove that we are better, faster, more economical and more conscious of our social and other responsibility. Metrics take performance out of the foggy realm of personal opinion into the bright light of objective assessment against standards. Metrics are what makes 'Professional', professional.

4. Faith

"When you come to the end of the light of all that you know and are about to step off into the darkness of the unknown, faith is knowing that one of two things will happen; there will be something firm to stand on or you will be taught how to fly." ~ Barbara Winters

This is my favorite quote that exemplifies for me the meaning of faith in terms of leadership. It is the willingness to go on when others have stopped. It is the belief, sometimes even 'irrational', that you will succeed. To believe that you will win and to show your commitment to this belief by continuing to go forward despite the lack of support. To go beyond what is 'reasonable' because in the end, it is the 'unreasonable' who win. Life is full of examples of great leaders who held on to their vision even in times of no support, only to be proven right when in the end they won. The South African anti-apartheid movement is a classic example of people fighting racism for decades in the face of tremendous opposition, firm in their belief that one day they would succeed. History is proof that they did. As I write this, there are others who take strength from this and other such examples and continue their struggle through the night of oppression.

This staying power, this psychological strength is essential and without it the best efforts fall by the wayside.

I discovered the power of prayer. Of asking the One who has the power for His help. Prayer gave me (and continues to do so) a chance to have a private conversation and to ask Allahﷻ for what I needed. He knew what that was better than I did, but being able to ask and knowing that He listens and helps gave me the strength that I needed.

There is an enormous sense of peace in standing in the night in prayer after having done all that is in one's power, asking for those decisions to be sent down without which all one's effort will bear no fruit. I am aware of the same sense of communion that the farmer feels when he has tilled the land, made the furrows, spread the fertilizer, sowed the seeds and then looks towards the heavens and raises his hands asking for rain, without which all his effort will be in vain. Yet when he raises his hands, there is no fear in his heart, only hope. And there is a smile on his face.

For he is looking for the clouds to come once again, bearing rain as they have done again and again in his life. So also as I stood, I remembered all the times that I had been guided, gently away from what I wanted, to what was good for me though I had not realized it at that time. I was aware that Allahﷻ knows, He cares and He has the power to do what it takes.

I was content in the fact that I had done my part and made all the effort that I could. Now I stood to ask for His help, confident that He would do what was good for me, even if it meant that in a given situation I would not get what I wanted. My life's experience told me that every time that happened I was given something better. Prayer gave me strength in the dark silence of the night which otherwise is the home of fear and confusion. I feel calmness and tranquility descend on me, my thoughts become clearer and new ideas emerge.

5. Deal with Ambiguity
Complexity is a source of profit

If there is one factor that is a certainty in all unique entrepreneurial ventures, it is ambiguity. The more path breaking your idea, the greater will be the number of things unknown. In most cases you will be the trend setter, the benchmark for those who come later, the poaching ground from where they will recruit their people.

Ambiguity creates anxiety and stress. I have two tools to deal with this:

1. Discipline and Routine

Anxiety creates disorder and disorder enhances fear. A vicious circle that debilitates energy and invites despair. So the first thing to ensure is that you have a routine and to stick to it with dogged discipline. I had (and continue to have) fixed times to wake up, sleep, eat and for all major activities including reading, writing and the gym. A timetable creates order and predictability in life.

Lack of discipline can masquerade as freedom. This is very dangerous. Structure is the most powerful aid to fight anxiety. Seriousness about work is not detrimental to having fun. The greatest fun is to win. Losing is very tragic.

2. Physical Fitness

Adrenalin is the best natural energizer. And you get a lot of it on the treadmill provided you sweat enough. The gym must become an absolutely fixed part of your day. Exercise is both a physical and psychological booster and a source of great benefit. Another thing, at least in my case, I think better when I am walking. So when I have some complex problem to work on, I go for a walk. By the time I have walked a few miles, I would have worked it out and it becomes clear. Whatever be the physiological reasons for this, I know it works for me. Try it out.

3. Resolve conflicts

Ambiguity creates multiple options and opinions. Multiple opinions create conflict. However this conflict if managed properly can become a binding force and create much better team cohesion. Also discouraging multiple opinions is a very good way to destroy all creativity and alternative thinking and hugely detrimental to eventual goal achieving.

So the first thing to realize and convince yourself as the leader is that conflict is desirable because it indicates that people are interested, engaged, concerned and see a stake for themselves in the outcome. It means that they see benefit for themselves in the task which is a very good sign.

Conflict resolution requires two things:
- Be aware of and able to deal with your own emotions

- Being able to deal objectively with issues

It is important to remember that you are also human and that in any conflict it is entirely possible that unconsciously you may prefer one side over another. However to show that or to allow that to influence you is detrimental to resolving the conflict. Emotion always gets in the way of resolution of conflict so though to feel emotion is entirely natural it is important to be able to control its expression and operate as objectively, dispassionately and fairly as you can.

To be able to do this, structure is a very major tool. So use structure to resolve conflicts. I use the following method:

1. Define the issue in terms of what is important to you.
2. Share the definition and identify common areas of agreement.
3. Agree on a mutually acceptable impartial, external, global standard.
4. Apply the standard and create a solution.
5. See if a better solution is possible.
6. Practice Active Listening (Paraphrasing)

It is very useful to keep the focus on the task and remind people not to become personal. There is a big difference between disagreeing and being disagreeable. Many people confuse a difference of opinion with opposition. This must not be allowed to happen or it will undermine relationships and destroy trust.

7. Execution

In the final analysis, it is the ability to deliver which is the game changer. Nothing else matters. Execution depends on two critical parameters:

1. Decision making

2. Edge

Decision Making

This has to do with the basis of decision making as well as the willingness to make decisions. Leadership after all is about the willingness and ability to take charge of other people's work and accept accountability for it. The worst self indictment of leadership is for the leader to complain about his team. So the leader's ability to take good decisions is a critical factor.

Good decisions are the result of applying systems as well as of systematically learning from experience. I want to emphasize the importance of systematic structured learning because not everyone who has a similar experience learns the same lessons. The value of the lesson depends more on how you learn than on what happened.

I use the following system:

1. Record what happened: hard data, recorded as dispassionately as possible.

2. Reflect on the reasons for it: and on what alternatives existed at the time.

3. Conceptualize a lesson: what do I learn from this?

4. Apply the lesson: with awareness.

It is a simple process the efficacy of which lies in the rigor with which it is applied. Many times we don't want to accept our own culpability in the issue; or we don't want to accept that we could have acted differently. So we don't learn anything and make the same mistakes again and again. But if we have the courage to look at our own actions and accept responsibility for them, then in fact we empower ourselves to create solutions. It is a strange paradox that when we accept responsibility for our own role in an incident, we simultaneously empower ourselves to change our future. As they say in Gestalt psychology:

'What I resist persists.
What I accept is transformed.'

Edge

To understand 'edge', imagine the edge of a knife. If you don't sharpen a knife then it needs far more force to cut and then cuts badly with ragged edges. We all know the old adage about sharpening the saw or sharpening the knife. Edge is about sharpening the knife of our decision making – the willingness and ability to take hard, painful decisions.

In my family business consulting practice I have seen case after case of business families refusing or unable to take hard decisions when it comes to succession, to the ultimate detriment, even destruction of the family business. One hard decision with respect to one individual, if not taken in time, leads to suffering and misery for the whole family. The strange thing is that this happens so many times.

An excellent example of the opposite – a hard decision taken at the right time – is the case of Pick 'n Pay Stores in South Africa founded by Raymond Ackerman. Not only did Ackerman plan succession for 25 years, as he says and has a record of every single succession planning meeting for all those years, when the time came for his own retirement, the top job did not go to his son Gareth

 but to Sean Summers, the CEO of the retail business. Gareth elected to oversee other family business interests. The interest of the business came first, over any aspirations to glory as the chairman of South Africa's premier retail business and the job went to the one who was considered best for it. Interestingly when Sean Summers resigned last week, his successor Nick Badminton was named immediately and smoothly, a proof of the effectiveness of Ackerman's succession planning philosophy. No vacuum, no searching, nobody from outside the organization. Talent identified and ready, waiting to take over.

Edge is critical to success for any leader. Without edge there can be no leadership. Some hard decisions are painful, but this pain is like the pain of cancer surgery – it saves the life. When you come to an edge decision, it is good to remember this example and remind yourself that death is even more painful. One last thing: a hard decision postponed, is harder to take and more painful when it is finally taken, perhaps too late.

As we have seen very clearly in the current (2009-10) economic slowdown, the recession happened because of financial indiscipline and unbounded greed. But strangely governments and regulatory bodies are reluctant to take hard decisions and instead have been pumping uncounted millions into systems which have failed so spectacularly. They don't seem to have heard of the phrase, 'throwing good money after bad'. As a result many months and a great many billions later there is no change visible in the scenery.

The same thing happens to a bad hiring decision. If you don't accept that you made a mistake and facilitate that mistake to make a career somewhere else, that mistake will multiply and become ever more difficult to correct.

1. Common Beliefs about the Interview

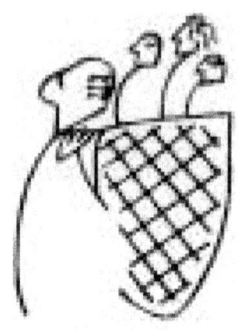

Below are some commonly held beliefs about interviewing. Please check 'True' or 'False' to show whether you agree or disagree with these statements.

1. In most cases the interview is a reliable tool for measuring a job candidate's skills.

2. Following your first impression generally pays off in interviewing.

3. Good interviewing is a matter of how good you are with people. It's an art that cannot be easily taught. `

4. Female applicants have an advantage over males since they have "women's intuition."

5. It makes good business sense to try people out, and if they don't work well, replace them. Fancy selection procedures are expensive and don't work well any way. Turnover is just an unavoidable cost of doing business.

6. Most interviewers are well aware of the shortcomings of the interview as a selection device.

7. The panel interview, with several interviewers and one candidate meeting at the same time should always be avoided. The panel interview puts unnecessary stress on the candidate and actually interferes with getting reliable information.

Research shows that all the above assumptions are false. The unstructured interview is about as effective in identifying real talent as throwing darts at a board on which you have written the names of the candidates. And a lot more expensive to do.

What is even more expensive as well as difficult to undo is the effect of the wrong hire. Like all hidden costs, the bad influence on the morale, attitudes and work culture that a loser has is very difficult to calculate. Finally like all partings, the pain of the eventual dismissal of the wrong hire leaves behind a taste that is not easily forgotten. The long and short of all this is that it is cheaper, more intelligent, more pleasant and far more effective to hire the right person in the first place.

Far more important than talent,
Is the courage to hire talent.

It is sad but true that many interviewers hire 'below' themselves. Some people feel 'threatened' by people more competent than themselves and will not hire them for that reason. Many times this is an unconscious thing and if the interviewer is not self-aware can result in him/her expressing even hostility to the candidate which naturally leaves the candidate confused.

Developing your own awareness is critically important in being able to conduct good and effective interviews.

In his famous book, Good to Great, Jim Collins says at the beginning of Chapter 3, *"When we began the research project we expected to find that the first step to taking a company from good to great would be to set a new direction, a new vision and strategy for the company, and then to get people committed and aligned behind the new direction. We found something quite the opposite. The executives who ignited the transformations from good to great did not first figure out where to drive the bus and then get people to take it there. No, they first got the right people on the bus (and the wrong people off the bus) and then figured out where to drive it. They said in essence, "Look, I don't really know where we should take this bus. But I know this much: If we get the right people on the bus, the right people in the right seats, and the wrong people off the bus, then we'll figure out how to take it someplace great."*

In more than 25 years of my practice as a Management Consultant and Executive Coach and Trainer and in 16 years as a hands-on line manager before that, if there is one thing that I have learnt, it is the truth of the above statement. When I first read it in Jim Collins book it was almost as if he had taken the words out of my mouth.

The key to greatness is the people. The right people who share our values and beliefs. And above all, who share our passion. Who are ignited by the same goals and who have the courage to dream bigger than we would ever dare. People who may be younger than we are but who we can look up to.

People whose aspirations make us lose sleep. People who scare us, because they challenge us to inspire them. And we know that to inspire them, we first have to break the boundaries of safety that we have gotten used to.

People who it is an honor and privilege to lead. To me, these are the 'right people'. Anything less would not be worth the effort or expense.

All of us have memories of working on teams where we  were excited. Where no goal was too big. Where big goals scared us but not into inaction or retreat but into renewed effort in the excitement of treading untrodden paths. Teams whose members became our best friends. People with whom we established lifelong friendship, long after the team itself was disbanded and we parted ways. It has been my privilege to have several such friends who started off as work colleagues. Some I hired. Others hired me. Still others simply worked together with me. All of them are dear friends long after our lives took us to different countries and companies and long after we stopped working together in a formal sense.

Right people. The whole secret is in hiring the right people. As they say, if you want someone to climb trees it is far better to hire a monkey than to train a rabbit.

10 – Reasons why the unstructured interview is as reliable as throwing darts at a board

As I mentioned earlier, the unstructured interview is a very unreliable method of hiring. There are lots of reasons why the typical interview has such a poor record as a predictive tool.

1. Most interviewers are not trained.

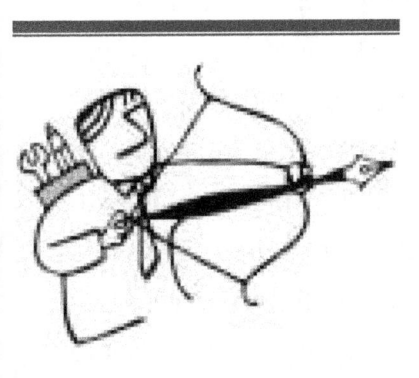

Like many areas of management, people are often just thrust into the job of interviewing when a vacancy needs to be filled. The need arises and they have to get on with it. So they do their best, but the organization pays the price of their mistakes in all sorts of insidious, damaging ways. Since neither the benefit of a right hire nor the cost of a wrong hire is ever formally measured, the extent of the real damage in damaged morale, sabotaged values, waste, inefficiency and a negative culture remains unknown. Interestingly the higher up the ladder the mistake is made the more the potential for damage.

2. Most people interview rarely, so they get very little practice.

If the successful candidate turns out to be a flop, it is rarely assumed that the interview was to blame. This means that the interviewer hardly ever gets specific feedback on what s/he did wrong. Most organizations don't even have the means to track the success or failure of the hire to the one who hired him. Nor is there any record of what actually happened in the interview. In many organizations it is culturally not acceptable to trace the success or failure of the hire to the hirer as it is seen as 'blaming' and embarrassing. So the interviewer does not know what s/he did wrong and never learns to do it right. Yet, it is a skill that can be improved by training, just like any other.

3. People often don't realize that they are bad at interviewing.

There are three things that people always seem to think they are good at - driving, parenting and interviewing. People believe that it is easy and natural. The fact is that like the others, it is neither. Interviewing is not instinctive and not 'natural' but is a skill that must be learnt. If we make an effort then we can indeed become very good at it. But the effort must be made. It is not difficult in itself but there are lots of mistakes that can be made, and training and practice help to avoid them. But if you don't think you need it, why bother to get trained? What must be kept in mind as I mentioned earlier is the cost of doing it wrong, which is both prohibitive and avoidable. That will encourage us to learn to interview well.

4. The typical interview generates a lot of information.

Untrained interviewers often find it very hard to sift the important information from the unimportant. How important is it that a candidate is assertive, for example?

One interviewer may see it as very important and so give it a lot of weight. Other interviewers may see it as less important or even as irrelevant, and so don't let this trait influence their judgment. The fact is that the relative importance of the trait or attitude or skill depends on the challenge of the job and the culture of your organization. It is critical therefore to standardize your questions so that you can get some comparable information. The typical interview question, "Please tell

 me something about yourself," is about the worst question to ask. Amazingly it is one of the most common.

5.   Very importantly, most selectors don't agree in a systematic way what skills, experience and qualities they are looking for in a person specifically.

So, since they are not all looking for the same things it's not surprising that they make different decisions on the same applicant. I am not trying to shut the doors to creativity or the potential benefit of unrelated experience. I am saying that in order to compare between candidates it is essential that we get information that (1) covers all critical areas and (2) that is comparable.

Once we have this basic information in a comparative manner then we can ask about whatever else we want to know without vitiating the process. It is also very important where more than one selector is involved (read 99% of interviews) that the selectors themselves are in agreement about what is required in the job as essential and what is desirable. The questions that are asked in the interview can then be molded on this basis to generate useful comparative data.

Lack of agreement among the interviewers is most detrimental.

6. Interviewers decide to accept or reject a candidate far too early in the interview, long before they have collected and considered all the evidence.

Many studies have shown that a typical interviewer makes up his or her mind about a candidate within the first three minutes of the interview. They then spend the rest of the interview finding evidence to support the decision they have already made. They seek out and remember good aspects of the candidate if they have decided to accept her and negative aspects if they don't want to take her on. This 'selective data gathering' can be proved even with what we read. I can show you how once you've made up your mind, you will actually not see contrary information that is written on the page you are reading. For example it has long been known about the Surgeon General's Warning against smoking printed in every larger letters on cigarette packets that smokers don't see it. It is essential in the interview therefore to ensure that you take cognizance of all the data, both that which confirms to your own likes and dislikes as well (and even more importantly) contrary data that goes against your first impressions.

7. Interviewers sometimes place more store by negative information than by positive evidence.

It is almost as if they are looking for reasons for rejecting a candidate, and if they don't find any then s/he must be OK. This is obviously not ideal. In some cultures where there's a premium on being self-critical, being critical of others has more value than being appreciative. In an interview this is counterproductive. What interviewers should be doing is neither being critical nor appreciative but they should collect good information which will help them to decide whether the applicant can and will adequately do the job they have in mind. Once again the primary reason for this is that most interviewers go into the interview unprepared. They don't know what they are looking for specifically. They haven't prepared specific questions to ask. They have not met earlier to agree on the essentials and desirables in the candidates. They have not read the resume and they have no standard method of asking or recording of data.

There is a cultural issue also where in many cultures, especially where unemployment is high, interviewees are seen as 'supplicants' and interviewers as 'givers'. Even though this may be factually correct in a purely economic sense, it remains equally true that you are not hiring people in order to provide employment. You are hiring them to fulfill some specific and important needs of your organization. An attitude of superiority is therefore counterproductive. You are not a gatekeeper to screen out 'undersirables' but a facilitator to ease the entry of 'desirables'. It is your role as a hirer that you identify the best talent and hire it. That is the only criterion. In this process naturally you will not hire those who are not suitable but that is merely the outcome of your search for the best.

8. Interviewers rarely change their minds about a candidate.

Please, go ahead keep talking..

RESUME

The biggest reason for this is that interviewers make up their minds too early in the game, as it were. Add to this the embarrassment of having to own up that perhaps you made a mistake; something that most people don't have the maturity to do. They would much rather insist on their original opinion and dig in their heels even when faced with data to the contrary. It is essential to remember that the interview is a place to gather data. Not a place to decide on the data. Once the data has been gathered, it must be considered, compared, discussed and then decided upon.

Two distinct processes which must be kept separate in order for the outcome to be effective.

Most people however, for a variety of reasons, collapse the two processes of data gathering and decision making together and so they take bad decisions even though they may well have had the data that would have saved them from that decision. This is also the most common reason for the false sense of urgency in many interviews where the interviewers feel themselves to be under pressure to decide one way or another.

It is essential to push back against this pressure, even if it exists, and tell those making the demand that in their own best interest, some patience is of the essence. Like in the hatching of eggs, if you simply increase the heat, the egg does not hatch faster but instead it gets cooked.

A reluctance to change your mind is also the result of a high opinion of one's own capability as a hirer which one then feels obliged to defend. The final test of the capability and competence of the hirer is the quality of the hire. If you hire winners consistently you are the best hirer. If not, you are a bad hirer, no matter what you think of yourself. It is like the batting average in cricket.

The number of runs you make in one match are not important. What is important is how you do in the whole tournament.

The best way to get the best result is to follow a systematic method that generates good data and enables you to come to the right decisions. Changing your opinion especially when data from the interview goes against it is a sign of maturity and commitment to the welfare of the organization. Unwillingness to change your opinion despite contrary evidence is a sign of an inflated ego and is detrimental to your role and organization.

9. Pressure interviews give false results

Pressure interviews, which thankfully are not used in the corporate world any longer (as far as I know) but are still the norm in government and the public sector are one of the worst ways to hire anyone. This is for two reasons: Pressure interviews favor extraverts and their extroversion can hide lack of depth and other fatal faults. Pressure is not the normal state of being in the workplace. So pressure tactics produce unnatural behavior which no matter how interesting and appealing it may seem in the interview room is not representative of what the candidate will do in real life.

Simulating the real thing as much as possible and using multiple means of assessment on the other hand is very useful.

10. Most interviewers rarely meet after the interview to compare and decide on data

Panel interviews are perhaps the most reliable tool that you can use provided the panel has a common set of agreed qualities they are looking for, have a prepared set of questions that they have asked, have taken notes and most importantly are willing to change their minds even to the extent of interviewing more candidates if they haven't found the ideal one.

In most organizations, instead of a panel a candidate is made to meet many people individually one after the other and then the decision is taken after the interviewers ask each other: What did you think of him/her?

There are clearly many things wrong with this process and it is almost programmed to give you the worst possible results. For example have you ever tried to repeat the same thing again and again, often in the same day? As the day progresses and you meet yet another person who asks you almost the same questions again, your energy flags, your irritation rises and you forget things. Believe it or not, the same thing happens to the poor interviewee. I have been on both sides of the table and so know this personally.

No matter how 'well trained' you consider yourself, our own prejudices, biases and preferences color our judgment. Some people like directness. Others find it threatening, impertinent or boastful. Some like to hear candidates talk about their achievements. Others like to hear the person say how his team helped him. Some like people who are 'pushy'. Others find them 'pushy'. We have our preference for a person's dressing, manner and appearance. Some like an orthodox, formal appearance. Others consider that to be an impediment and potential problem. That is why it is very beneficial when interviewers meet face to face and have a chance to compare notes about a candidate because they can correct each other's prejudices and see facts in a more objective manner.

Most often however, once the interview is over, the interviewers compare notes by phone and ask, 'What did you think of so-and-so?' Please notice, in this question that there is no comparison of data from the questions which each one asked, which would have been really useful. There is no comparison of notes – assuming that they were taken. There is no examination of assumptions of individual interviewers. There is no questioning of conclusions based on common evidence (there is no common evidence anyway). They are merely asking the 'opinion' of the other person without any understanding about why they formed that opinion. All this leads to a situation where the benefit of the opinion of several people is lost and wrong conclusions are drawn, completely unnecessary.

If you take the trouble of doing a panel interview which I strongly recommend you to do, then please complete the process by comparing notes face to face without which the benefit of the panel interview will be lost and you would have taken all that trouble to no avail.

Self Test

Please read the statements below and say if you consider them 'True' or 'False'. Please don't read the answers until you finish scoring.

1. The untrained interviewer's personality may contribute as much to the outcome of the selection decision as to do the characteristics of the candidate.
2. The interview is a sample of behavior.

3. First impressions can mislead the interviewer.

4. Every interview will contain some subjectivity that influences decision-making.
5. The interview is biased only if done by a biased person.
6. The best predictions of job performance come from descriptions of underlying personality factors.
7. People are constantly changing, so their behavior won't be much help in predicting their future actions.
8. To predict people's behavior, we need to know what

motivates them, and what they want out of life.

9. There is a lot of sense in the saying, "Birds of a feather flock together." By knowing about a candidate's friends and relations, we can get a good idea of his or her performance potential.

10. The candidate says, "I'm good with people", causing the behavioral interviewer to predict that he will do well in a customer relations job.

11. In the trait of approach, descriptions of traits are accepted as valid, while in the behavioral approach they are used s the basis for probes to elicit behavioral examples.

12. Non-verbal behavior is ignored in the Behavioral interview, since it is an unreliable guide to a candidate's personality.

Answers

1. **True**   Research supports that the Interviewer unconsciously selects, omits and interprets the data to fit expectations based on the Interviewer's own personality and background.

2. **True**   The interview is a very small sample of behavior and the Interviewer must be skilled to make it as representative of the candidate as possible.

3. **True**   The first impression can cause the Interviewer to select, omit and interpret information to confirm a gut feeling.

4. **True**   All people make predictable errors in judgment. Any task relying on judgment will reflect

some subjectivity. The goal of structured interviewing is to reduce subjectivity.

5. **False** All people have biases, and all judgment is reflected by bias. It is important to protect the candidate from even unconscious biases.

6. **False** Research consistently shows that past and present behaviors are the best predictors of future behavior. What one has done in the past is the best indicator of what one will do in the future.

7. **False** While people do change, patterns of behavior do offer a valuable basis for predicting future actions.

8. **False** Current or past behavior is a better predictor of future behavior than any abstract trait or personality description. For example, what you want out of life does not typically relate to the skills that are important for a particular job.

9. **False** Stereotypes do not help us rate an individual's skills for a particular job. In fact, asking

about friends or family may fall into the category of an illegal question.

10. **False**   The Interviewer makes predictions based on past behavior, not on self-described traits. The Interviewer will probe for a specific example that would provide evidence about the candidate's actual skill in dealing with people.

11. **True**   The Interviewer uses trait responses as a cue to ask for real life examples.

12. **False**   Non-verbal behavior IS used by the Interviewer to generate new questions and to check for consistency with verbal behavior. However non-verbal behavior ALONE is insufficient for predicting future behavior.

Naturally all this takes time; one of the major 'objections' to the structured interview. But then the way I put it is, "If you want a baby you have to wait 9 months." There is an organic time to achieving results. Accurate results. Your call if you want accurate results or not. There are no shortcuts, believe it or not.

True it is that one can accelerate some processes but equally true, is that if you accelerate a process beyond what it is capable of achieving you only shortchange yourself. I am not suggesting that there is a magic number in terms of the amount of time a good interview must take. However I do believe that more the potential impact of the person you are hiring and the greater the potential harmfulness of a hiring mistake, the more time must go into the interview. With this in mind I would say that an interview for any leadership position must take the best part of an hour at the very least.

Given that the cost of the individual may well cross a hundred thousand dollars and a mistake in hire may well be worth many times that in direct and indirect costs, spending an hour is hardly too long. You may take the help of others to screen candidates before they come to you but you must spend the time when it is your turn.

You <u>can't</u> tell a book by its cover.

There is a famous proverb in English, 'You can tell a book by its cover.' I believe that when assessing people the opposite is true. You CAN'T tell a book by its cover. People can and do tailor their appearance and presentation to suit your known preferences, likes or culture. On the other hand there are non-conformist individuals who look very different from your 'ideal candidate' but they may well be that game-changing person you need to revolutionize your business. The hiring interview is a serious exercise with long lasting impact. That is why it is essential to ensure that you read the whole book as it were, before buying it. Not simply look at the cover.

First impressions are long lasting but are often wrong. After we have known someone for a while we may have reason to revise the first impression. The problem with the typical interview is that we don't have the luxury of several months of acquaintance before we make up our mind. So the first impression can color our view such that we make serious hiring errors. Appearances can be tailored to suit your known preferences (IBM = Light shirt + dark tie. Apple = No tie) and 'educated' candidates often do their best to fit in with your organization's known culture. The same is true of language and demeanor.

We also tend to like people who are more like us and from a background similar to our own (school, country, race, place, language, accent, religion, economic status). This can lead to major faults in judgment and very often to wrong selection. It is said, and not without reason, that most untrained interviewers, in a one hour interview, make up their minds in the first 3 minutes and then spend the next 57 minutes, justifying their choice. **So beware of first impressions.**

So what is a hiring interview and how is it different from other meetings?

Interviewing is neither a form of deception, persuasion nor entrapment, but the art of asking questions whose responses yield pertinent assessment data. The key to interviewing is to ask 'good' questions.

In this book you will learn how to do that. You will learn the difference between a good and a bad question. And you will learn how to ask the questions that will yield the kind of data you need in order to make an accurate assessment of the person.

It is very important to remember this. Often people go into interviews almost as if they were there as investigating detectives with the task of 'tripping up' the candidate or 'catching' them in a lie.

Please remember that this is an interview and not an interrogation and that you are not a detective and the candidate is not a suspect. Our role as interviewers is to create an atmosphere of comfort and frankness where we can each assess the other's suitability to their needs:

the candidate's as a prospective employee and our own as a prospective employer.

Just as it is highly desirable for you, the hiring manager to know everything about a candidate in order to make a wise decision, it is equally important and something that in the long run will save you a lot of grief, if the candidate can also get an accurate picture about what it will be like for him to work in your organization. Not a 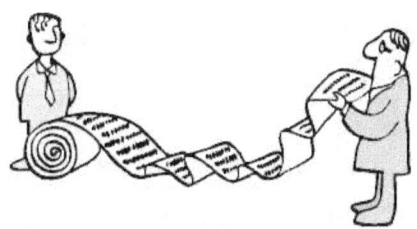 wishful 'sales pitch' but the real facts. That way s/he can decide if they fit in and save you a lot of trouble.

The best way to predict what a candidate <ins>will do</ins> is to look at what they did before they came to you. One can have many aspirations but behavior is the only thing that can be seen and measured.

The structured interview which probes a person's previous experience and arrives at what they have done in the past is the best way to predict what they can/are likely to do in the future. A person may have all the good intentions in the world, but unless you want to provide them the opportunity to experiment on your time and at your cost, there is no guarantee that what they intend to do, they can actually implement. While I am all in favor of risk taking and providing an atmosphere of experimentation for people to live their dreams, one thing I can say for sure; that there is no guarantee that you are going to get the results that you are hiring for. If you have the time and money to permit experimentation, that's fine. Otherwise you are taking a chance and it is a good thing to know that.

You may get the genius who will revolutionize your business. But more than likely you are going to get people who will disappoint you and waste your time and resources simply because there are ten turkeys for every genius. The only guarantee that someone will do/can do something is when we see evidence of their having done it before. That is why pilots have to put in several hundred hours of solo flight before they are allowed into the cockpit of your plane. And you are very happy that this is so. I don't think you'd like to be flying on a plane that is to be piloted by someone whose lifelong dream has been to fly a plane but who has never flown solo before. Sure, there's always a first time and people don't crash on every first solo flight.

But the operative question is do you want to be in the passenger's seat?

One word of explanation – when I say, 'What has a person done before?' – the purpose is to get actual hard data on his/her achievements, behavior, reactions and responses. Remember, it is not our job to understand (as a psychoanalyst does) why people behave the way they do in terms of the underlying drives and motivations. All we need to be able to do is to get substantiated information about what they have done in the past in order to predict what they are likely to do in the future.

For example if a person is known to throw things at others when s/he is angry, it is not our role to understand the factors leading to expression of anger in that manner or what in the person's childhood or youth led to this particular manifestation of behavior. It is enough to know that they do this when they are angry so that we can wear a helmet when we meet them in that state.

In this process, often a person's failures are more educative than their successes. How a person behaves in failure is a very good measure of his character. Did he display resilience, fortitude and courage?

Or did he run away. What were his learnings from his failures? Can you find some evidence that he worked out solutions to the problems which means they will not be repeated?

Successes also must be probed for learnings. Sometimes people have glowing track records because they lived in good times and worked in good companies. The market was good; she worked for a stable, professional, process driven organization and had a stellar career. The CV looks fantastic and you are hugely impressed. You are a startup which is now in its second stage funding and staffing. You are looking to induct 'good people from multinationals who can bring in systems'. So you hire this person who has this brilliant career, without asking, 'How many of the systems that she used in her organization does she really have knowledge of from a design perspective?' Or what is this person likely to do when they don't have the support of the systems of a large multinational behind them? Or what is their attitude to getting their hands dirty and making their own coffee? The result of such hires is self evident. There is a difference between a BMW driver and a BMW mechanic. If you want your car fixed, you'd better hire a mechanic and not a driver.

Similar is the case with graduates of big name schools, especially business schools with one additional element; he will have the language and the coaching to attend interviews. On the other side he will have at best experience of simulations and case studies which is certainly the best way we know to teach as on date but is still a far cry from the real thing. Imagining a crisis and thinking of a response to it is not even a shadow of being in a crisis and coming out alive.

I am saying all this not because I have anything against business schools; I went to one of the best myself and teach at several others; but because I have seen hiring managers hire shining new MBA's, put them to work in situations where experience counts more than anything else and then be very disappointed when the poor guy fell apart.

That is why while interviewing it is essential to keep your eyes wide open both with respect to what you really need and what the candidate can realistically be expected to provide. Hire new graduates by all means but give them the experience they need before you put them to the test.

Cost of Hiring the Best

To appreciate the real value of hiring Winners, it is useful to calculate the cost of hiring Losers.

What is the cost of a wrong hire?

- Cost of paying for non-performance?
- Cost of replacement?
- Cost of lost opportunity?
- Cost of the detrimental effect on others?
- Cost of damaged image/morale?
- Cost of bruised/lost customers?

The cost of wrong hiring is never calculated in most organizations and so like all such hidden costs, wrong hires keep bleeding the reputation, profitability and morale of your organization, often with near terminal effects. The cost of damage control and repair can be prohibitive and in some cases the damage can be irreversible in terms of lost customers or reputation. The real tragedy is that all this could easily have been avoided with a little bit of care in hiring.

Another factor that is not measured is the fact that most people hire less competent people than themselves. Many people are afraid of people more competent than they are because they fear for their own jobs. In many cases this is a hidden fear that they will never admit to but it operates very strongly while hiring. In many organizations many old timers have simply grown into jobs that they are not really expert in. This is especially true where the present day job needs a high degree of technical input and many older people are not techno-savvy and unwilling to learn new things. So they keep stalling and hire people who don't 'frighten' them. This usually translates as incompetence. This is a very serious mistake.

It is essential for the growth and development of the organization that we hire high performers. High performers raise the bar. They make demands which enforce learning. They push the limits of 'possibility'. They make the impossible, possible. But they have to be hired first and then supported and encouraged, even challenged to be better than they thought they were. Exceptional hiring managers are those who can recognize quality that is superior and hire it. But like all things exceptional, they are not common.

It is well known that it is more difficult to motivate high performers than to motivate pedestrians. It is this factor that puts pressure on the superiors who have to justify their 'superiority' by inspiring respect. This is especially true when we consider the fact for example, that what we learned in Engineering College, the kids we hire today, 30 years later, probably read about that in history class in school. So they actually know more than we do and that is the reason we hire them. Yet we still have to inspire them and be role models to them. However this pressure is very good to have as it constantly enhances the capability of the organization. This is what I call 'Positive Stress'. Hiring high performers is the cheapest and most cost effective way to do this. But how do we define a High Performer? And how do we distinguish him or her from the one who may be good enough but is not outstanding?

Here's a tool to differentiate between 'satisfactory' and 'outstanding'.

Satisfactory	Excellent	Outstanding
Performs to the level expected of a fully qualified and experienced person. Sometimes performs with excellence. Fulfills objectives with accuracy and in time. Requires minimal supervision. Manager has confidence in his/her performance & recommendations.	Accomplishment above expected levels, sustained & consistent. Performance exceeds position requirements. Achieves thorough, on-time results with little direction. Seeks challenging goals and achieves them. Decisions and actions are always in line with organization values and support the culture.	Far exceeds normal expectations on a sustained basis; seldom equaled in overall contribution. Takes initiative to transfer knowledge, trains others and is seen as a leader. Takes initiative in identifying challenging goals & maximizing results. Thinks beyond the immediate job and seeks to identify new business opportunities.

It can be empirically measured and proven that 'Excellent' people may cost a little more but produce results which are far superior.

What is not so easily measured but perhaps even more important is the effect of outstanding individuals on the culture of the organization. Like magnets outstanding people attract others like themselves. They nurture greatness and rejoice in seeing their subordinates excel their own performance. They look out of the window to give credit. They look in the mirror when it comes to owning responsibility. Outstanding people demand

outstanding results. They are not satisfied with mediocrity. They are difficult to satisfy and even more to delight. They can be seen as 'pushy' and their own internal drive as 'exhausting'.

Customers on the other hand will benchmark your organization by the outstanding people in it. For them, these are the face of your organization. They come to you because they can deal with such people who not only give them what they need but surprise them with things that they did not know were possible. They experience value for money that ordinary people could never hope to give and for that reason, they are loyal to you.

Remember, people don't work for organizations, they work for other people. And customers of everything other than off the shelf soap or toothpaste don't buy from organizations, they buy from other people. No matter which industry or business you are in, no matter how technical or automated it is, somewhere along the line there is a human being, and he or she is critically important. If that person is outstanding, you have an outstanding business. If that person is a pedestrian, you have a mediocre business on its way to becoming history.

Outstanding people create and reinforce a culture of accountability, professional pride, striving for excellence and the joy of achieving results that others did not think were possible. These are the people who dare to go where none have gone before. They are the pioneers who attract followers. They create inspiration. That is one reason why companies like GE, Merck, Toyota and Sony attract the best people in the market even though they don't pay the highest salaries. People like to work for these companies for the opportunity to work with great people. They know that the experience is worth more than a college degree and will give their career a boost

that no college can. The best thing about outstanding people is that mediocre people either improve or leave. Any organization that is serious about becoming great one day needs such people as much an individual needs blood in his veins. Aiming low and being satisfied with hiring mediocre people is a very expensive choice to make, more so because unlike material assets, people can't simply be removed from the shelf if you discover that you made a mistake. Mediocre people don't cost less; they cost far more than outstanding people. It is their value however which is far less. Remember, cost and value are two different things. Without outstanding people your organization is condemned to a path of mediocrity and oblivion.

Winners attract people like themselves.
Losers do the same.

Finding Winners

Winners are found in the most unexpected places. They have the most unexpected profiles. Many of them don't fit the standard profiles that we are used to seeing. The largest employers in the business world today are people who would not be eligible for a $250 per week job. And thank god for that. Otherwise, Reliance, Microsoft, Dell, Sony and other organizations like them would not exist. They were all founded by people who did not fit the standard profile. They were started by people who followed their dreams often in the face of opposition. But they were all started by winners. Many winners were slow starters. Others took chances and risks which involved doing non-traditional things and stepping out of the box. Many dropped out of college because the traditional method or material taught did not excite them. This does not mean that every college drop-out is outstanding but that some outstanding people drop out of traditional schooling. It is not the reason you will select them but also not the reason you will discard their resume because you see a 'gap' in education. Remember, sometimes the most valuable lessons we learn are not in school. Outstanding people are not like everyone else. However that is the definition of outstanding – not like everyone else.

The first rule in hiring winners is not to limit yourself to the resumes that your placement agent can send you. Use your contacts and network, both social and professional. But in the urge to find good people, please beware of breaking unwritten ethical hiring rules. Poaching is decidedly unpleasant when done to us and you can rest assured that it is equally unpleasant when we do it to others. And in the end it comes home to roost as so many new companies in India in the early days of the IT and BPO boom found to their own cost. Loyalty is a good old value that is still good today.

However there is no harm in hiring someone who has already left a competitor and is on the lookout for a job. Your own conscience is a good guide to decide what the dividing line between honesty and wrong practice is.

Encouraging dishonesty directly or indirectly only spoils the whole atmosphere for everyone, raising cost, encouraging disloyalty, focus on money alone, devaluing work culture and learning, raising anxiety and stress and lowering trust all around. Some organizations play these games where they talk all about loyalty, learning, human value and whatnot but when it comes to hiring they look only at money. This creates a corresponding culture among the people who all listen with their eyes and pay little heed to all the exalted talk when they can see that all that counts is money. I am not against money. I am against the dishonesty and hypocrisy which many organizations deal in. Say it like it is and stop pretending.

If you want people to work for you for reasons other than money, then let them join you for reasons other than money. Focus on why they want to leave the other organization. Maybe right in the middle of your most critical project they may want to leave you for the same reason, leaving you in the lurch as they did your competitor. Chickens roost at home. The IT and BPO industries in India are currently suffering from this and their appalling attrition rates are directly related to the nasty climate that they created for themselves.

The Staffing Challenge:

What to do when you have a job open.

The first thing to do when a job falls vacant is to actively and consciously decide if it needs filling at all. There may well be an opportunity to eliminate that job and enrich other jobs related to it by reallocating the responsibilities. This is especially true of companies in  the growth phase. Many jobs were created in the start-up phase simply because something had to be done and if you had someone to do it; you had to call him something to be able to pay him. So the job got created. Nobody bothered about where it fit into the greater scheme of things or what career path the individual would have. In the start-up phase there simply isn't the time or inclination to think of all these things. However as time passes and an organization gets built, these questions become progressively more essential to address. Simply filling a vacant job therefore is not advisable.

It is essential before filling the vacancy to ask if the position itself is still necessary. Maybe it is now far cheaper and more efficient to outsource that job or to mechanize it and eliminate one position from your own headcount.

If you do decide that the job must be filled, take some time to reassess the requirements for the job. It is an eye-opener sometimes to look at the job requirements in the light of changed realities of the job even though the title may still be the same.

For example the job title **'Administrative Manager'** may still be the same as it was when the current incumbent was hired, 20 years ago. However when you are filling his position today, you will certainly need to hire someone with a very different skill set. Technology and how well someone understands it is often a major consideration. So also the new spectrum of constituents that a modern Administrative Manager will need to be able to deal with will demand communication and social skills that someone 15 or 20 years ago did not need. The way employee unions have changed and so has the profile of the union leader is a good case in point.

Language and style which worked when the union leader was either a local petty politician or a shop floor worker with some leadership skills, will spell disaster today where the union leader has a Masters degree in social science and a post graduate degree in law. Many people don't take the time to list the new skills, experience and talents they will need today and hire someone like the one who left. Such mistakes are expensive but easily avoidable.

 While creating this specification list however, please beware of listing unattainable parameters. It is very easy to give-in to the temptation of writing a wish list which is unrealistic. This is counterproductive as even if you are able to find the kind of person you dreamed up, he/she will probably quickly get disillusioned as they are not able to find the satisfaction and challenge that they need. Being realistic is essential. This does not mean that you should not be ambitious and aim a little higher than you need, but beware of asking for qualifications and skills that you may not be able to use in the foreseeable future.

Hire Values & Attitude, Train Skills

Differentiate between what you need to hire and what you can train-in. I believe that the best bet is to hire values and attitude and train people in the behavior and skills that they need. It is true that people have changed their attitudes and literally transformed, but remember that we talk about them because they are the exception. Most attitudes and all values are hard wired; developed from infancy through to early adulthood and remain the same. Changing them often requires surgery. Most organizations have neither the skills nor the time to invest in this kind of change and eventually have to resort to firing the individual usually after a painful existence. But how are you to know if an individual actually has an attitude or believes in the value that he claims to do? After all nobody will say, 'I don't really believe in integrity,' or some such thing.

The secret is some homework. You need to develop 'Operative definitions' for each value/attitude which you are looking for. An Operative Definition is a description of behavior which will tell you if the individual actually practices that value of has that attitude or not. Without a clear Operative Definition you have to take the person's word for it.

For example if you are looking for someone who is a quick learner and self motivated to develop his or her own competence, you would probe for a regular pattern of learning that the individual has paid for himself. If you find it, it will tell you that here's someone who is interested enough in his own development to put his own money where his mouth is. Someone whose learning is restricted to company organized training programs is obviously not the kind of person you are looking  for even if he is trained well enough. It is your Operative Definitions which will guide you to the questions you need to ask to ascertain the facts. That is why the homework is important.

Values are important because Values drive behavior and Behavior drives results. Factor in the time it will take to train. Sometimes depending on urgency it may be faster to hire than to train. At other times, training is the more cost effective option.

As I mentioned earlier, values, beliefs (which effect behavior) and attitudes must be hired. They are almost impossible to train-in and whereas some attitudes can be changed, the process is painful and difficult. It is simpler to screen for these things and hire people who have them already. The same is true of social skills and manners which though they can be trained, the process is messy. Also manners are a matter of upbringing which in the workplace you neither have the time nor the ability to do.

All skills and behavior can be trained. And so also some attitudes, like Customer Orientation, Results Orientation and so on. But other attitudes like a hunger to win, (Achievement Motivation) the internal pressure for constant self improvement (Self Learning) are very difficult to train. People either have them or they don't. We hear many stories of people recruiting on planes and trains but sensational news apart, it is in fact true that if you keep an eye open you can find excellent people in unexpected places.

The old British tea companies understood this principle – Hire Values/Attitudes, Train Skills – very well and practiced it with great success. I recall with amusement my first job interview with the Kannan Devan Tea Company (now Tata Tea) in Munnar, Kerala.

I was asked to report one day prior to the date of the interview. An old friend, who was an Assistant Manager and knew the ropes, told me that this was to see if the candidates would fit the social scene. I was to wear a tie and lounge suit, he said. We, all those who had been called for the interview, would start in the Men's Bar in the High Range Club and after the drinks were over, we would be invited into the dining room to have dinner which we would have all together. While we did this, different people would come and talk to us. And all this would be observed and would count in our favor or against us in the interview the next day.

Sure enough that evening we were asked to present ourselves at the High Range Club, sharp at 7.00 pm. About 12 of us in various styles of suits and ties found ourselves in the Men's Bar (Sign said: Women not permitted). We were asked what we drank. When it came to my turn, I said that I would like to have a soft drink. People looked at me with various expressions; the barman with pity, fellow contestants with derisive smiles, and other inhabitants of the bar with a variety of expressions related to whether they thought I was a poor fool, uncultured or just plainly idiotic. To put the record straight, someone in the meanwhile gave me the drink that I wanted.

As I sat there (I was all of 18 years old) wondering about the job that I had applied for and what drinking alcohol had to do with it, I heard a loud, "Hello there!" I looked up to see a florid red face in a body without a neck and a large smile, looking at me. I stood up and greeted him to which he responded cordially and we shook hands. "So you don't drink, eh?" he asked. Seeing that I was drinking a fresh lime soda (what else can you do with an FLS?) and that he could see what I was doing, I decided to keep silent and simply smiled and nodded. Smiling and nodding is an excellent strategy to allow people to interpret whatever they want. "Tell me something young fellow," he said, "Do you play cricket?" I said that I did but other people who played with me, wished that I didn't. Then he asked me, "Are you a Mason?" At that time, not being aware of the Free Masons and the

Masonic Lodge, I thought he wanted to know if I could build walls. "No, I'm not," I said.

He looked me up and down with a funereal expression on his face and said, "You don't drink, you don't play cricket and you are not a Mason. Boy! You don't have a chance."

Then looking at my face once again (I guess I looked shocked), he said in a reassuring tone, "Anyway, don't worry, I am not on the recruitment panel." As it turned out, he wasn't but his thinking was. Reflecting on this incident, what is clear to me is the principle behind this method. In a place with a limited population (you did not count the estate staff and God Forbid, the workers as people) that you could socialize with, it was essential that you hired people who were socially acceptable. So social values and training had overwhelming importance. The skills of tea plantation management were all trainable. On the other hand, eating at table using the right fork for the right meat, drinking yet not getting drunk, making conversation that was inane yet interesting, dancing with the manager's wife and so on were all skills that were either thought to be not trainable or too much trouble. So British managers (including their acolytes, the Brown Sahibs) hired young people from backgrounds which were socially acceptable to them and then trained them for job related skills, on the job.

To close the loop and take you out of your suspense I was not hired. The Sahib's prediction was right, even though he was not on the panel. Brown sahib's were always more conscious of snobbery anyway. And who wanted a fellow who neither drank nor played cricket or had any inclination to lead substantial ladies through their moves?

Mercifully today we have come a long way from this situation and drinking and dancing are no longer core values. However the principle still holds true – Hire Values/Attitudes, Train Skills.

The Resume

The first introduction to the candidate is the resume. It is important to make the best use of this which sometimes due to pressure of numbers we don't do. Here is a tool to help you to scan resumes such that you can get the essential information that you need from them.

Resume screening tool

It may be useful to keep this handy when you read resumes especially as skillful resume writers can often disguise what you want to see and highlight what they want you to see. Missing details can be costly waste of time. Getting people to apply in a standard form that you have designed is a good idea so that you can get some comparable data.

Experience/Education

- What they did is often more important than where they did it. Schools, locations and previous employers can all have an influence that overshadows the actual achievement of the individual. So if someone comes from a great company, you may be inclined to hire them even if they don't have the critical experience you need. Needless to say, actual work experience is the only guarantee that they can deliver results.

Gaps/void in date continuity

- Why the gap? What did they do in the gap? The gap itself is not necessarily a disqualification. Just that you want to probe to see what the individual did in that time. If they used it in constructive ways, then the gap may actually be in their favor.

Career progress in relation to time taken.

- Why fast or slow? What does it say about expectations today? In a world that is changing very fast, people have different expectations about the speed of progress in their careers. Where in the old days to become a 'people manager' took anything between 7-10 years, today in a BPO it can take as little as 2 years. That is not to say that the 2 year old 'people manager' has the wealth of people management experience that 7 years of IR, managing a unionized workforce can give you. But s/he may still have expectations of becoming a VP the following year. This also shows that merely changing designations mean nothing. It is the depth, scope and complexity of experience which must be probed for.

Actual results achieved

- What they personally did, not what the team, company or industry did. Like the story of the ant and the elephant, the bridge shook because the elephant crossed it. Not because the ant was sitting on his back. You need to identify if the resume belongs to the ant or the elephant.

Career /employer changes

- Why did they change? Reasons for changing are most important as they give a window into the candidate's attitude to challenges. Some people are quitters. Others are perpetual gold diggers. Whereas one can't really hold someone's desire to get a better salary against them, it is essential that you hire people who are interested in their work, have some long term plans to contribute and are motivated by the culture of your organization. Reasons for change of employers and career choices can give you pointers towards this.

Lengths of time on jobs

- Especially if too long or too short. The time period may also be influenced by the industry, but do ask the questions. Low mobility can be a sign of low competence and political skill. It can also be a sign of loyalty and steadiness. High mobility can be a sign of instability or high political skill or of a high achiever who needs strong leadership to inspire him or her. The time they spent on the job, especially when related to what they achieved can give you pointers to their suitability.

It is good to keep this list handy when reading resumes. It is quite easy sometimes to get influenced by the name of a college or a previous employer when he / she may actually not meet some criteria on this list.

Pushing back on time pressure

All hiring managers and all HR Managers who are hiring are under pressure. Line Managers often act as if hiring managers are magicians and new employees can be pulled out of a hat like the magician's rabbit. No matter how much you understand the reality of the line manager it is difficult to keep your cool and focus on doing a good job at the same time. Expecting delays and pressures helps in keeping frustration at bay.

It is realistic to assume that sometimes you may have to give in to some pressures of time and exigencies of work and as long as you don't feel that you are compromising on basic values of the organization or your own, it is acceptable to hire for the short term. Wrong hiring is not only expensive but it will bring you back to square one that much faster.

My thumb rule however, when I agree to hire for the short term is to ensure, that I know exactly why I am agreeing and what I am going to do with that employee after the immediate need is over. Firing them is not the ethical thing to do in such cases.

It is very important to have an overall business focus and not think only in terms of your own unit. You may come across an outstanding candidate that does not fit your bill but may be very useful in another part of the business. Remember that quality is not a onetime thing. Quality is an all time thing. Quality is infectious and self propagating. Quality begets quality and so it is worth searching for, worth waiting for and worth paying for. I know of many instances where people went for what was cheap even though it was low quality and lived to regret their decision when the final bill came up and they realized the real cost of poor quality. But I don't know of a single instance where someone hired a top quality person and regretted it.

I am reminded of the Gucci family slogan, **'Quality is remembered long after the price is forgotten.'** That applies not only to shoes and handbags. It applies to people even more because unlike shoes and bags people influence other people, they create an image, they make or mar your reputation, they impact customers, they are your face and in the end, they will spell your success or failure.

To those being hired

I think it is not out of place to offer some advice to those aspiring to be hired. Many go to courses that seem to focus almost entirely on how to show the best side of yourself and somehow get yourself hired. They talk about what to wear and how to walk into the interview room and tell you stories of their friend who stumbled and fell flat on his face as he entered the room. Then stood up, dusted himself and said, 'Good morning gentlemen. It appears I have fallen into good company.' And he was hired.

Well, nice story. However if he was only hired for that one line then the story is a good illustration of how not to hire. Dress, appearance, demeanor, a smile on the face, a firm handshake and a ready tongue are all useful and desirable but in the end one must focus on what the candidate has to offer in terms of experience and ability to deliver results if you want to be successful.

The real issue is that it is not only your best side that is being hired but your whole self. And if there is a worse side to you, then it is bound to cause you grief later down the road if you keep it hidden during the interview. This applies also to overpromising and claiming to be able to do things that you really have no experience of. I have seen many over enthusiastic people make such claims and then flounder when the time came to deliver results.

So what should you do?

Honesty is still the best policy, even to this day. Be frank and clear. I am not advocating that you volunteer all kinds of deeply emotional information about all your childhood anxieties and fears. I mean, be clear about what you can do and what you can't. Even if you don't want to volunteer information about what you can't do to begin with, do seek information about the job you are interviewing for and if you believe there is something in it that is not in your experience, then talk about it.

You can say that you are willing to learn, but the interviewer must understand that there is likely to be some learning time before you can be expected to deliver results. Talk about what you have done ensuring that you mention clearly what you did personally and what others on your team did. That way the interviewer can see what your own ability is as well as see that you are someone who is willing to give credit to others. Believe me that will cut a lot more ice than someone pretending that the sun shines because of him.

Talk about your successes and what you learnt from them. Equally importantly talk about your failures and what you learnt from them. Don't hide failures because if you can show that you learnt from them, they will give you a lot of credit. Someone who is willing to talk about where they failed and what they learnt from that leaves the listener with much more mental comfort than someone who claims never to have failed. Remember that it is the learning that is important in both success and failure. That is why this is something that you need to spend some time thinking about and preparing before you go to the interview. It is entirely likely that in the tension of the interview you may forget some useful data which would have done you a lot of good if only you had prepared in advance. It is a good idea to make some notes for yourself. Don't trust your memory. It is never as good as we think.

Be polite. Thank the interviewer for his time. Make eye contact and speak clearly and not too fast. Be aware of the interest level in the person listening to you. Sometimes many technical people get so engrossed in

intricate detail that the interviewer goes brain-dead listening to him. If you see that the interviewer is about to expire it is a good idea to stop talking about your beloved widget.

Once the interviewer has finished asking his questions, be sure to ask your own. Have these prepared in advance so that you don't leave the place and then regret not having asked about some vital detail. Remember however that the seasoned interviewer will also assess you by the kinds of questions that you ask. So don't ask about information that is available on the company website. Read the website in detail before you go to the interview and make your notes.

Ask about growth plans. Ask about what the interviewer sees as key challenges, especially with respect to your job. Share your thoughts about what you see as the challenges that face the organization and ask about their plans to meet those challenges. That will demonstrate your own competence and that you did your homework. If you have ideas about what you think will work, volunteer to share them. If the interviewer seems interested then talk. For example you may say, 'On that count, I have thought of a strategy that will work. Glad to talk about it when you have some time.' Then leave it to the interviewer to encourage you. I have yet to see a shrewd manager refuse to listen to some potentially good ideas. Naturally you'd better have something useful to say if you are given the chance.

Finally what not to do. Don't joke. Smile but don't crack jokes. Some can backfire very badly and destroy your credibility. Be aware of and sensitive to the culture of the organization and country. If you see that the interviewer is a Muslim man or woman and you are of the opposite gender, don't offer to shake their hand. If you are a man, put your right hand on your heart and bow in greeting. It is graceful, extremely polite and she'll appreciate that very much. If you are a woman then just greet verbally. That is enough and will also be appreciated. In Eastern cultures, don't point your feet at the interviewer either by extending your legs or by placing your foot on your knee. It is considered very impolite. Use 'Sir' or 'Madam' and don't use first names unless asked to do so. Being extra polite never hurt anyone. The opposite does.

Create a Hiring Template

The hiring template is in two parts. One is the **Technical Skills** part and the other is the **Attitudes or Values** part. Time spent in doing a good job of creating a useful template eliminates a lot of wasted time in post-interview assessment. A template ensures that you are clear about the critical requirements of the job which a candidate must have. It also helps you to comparatively assess the relative value of different candidates more objectively. In any case it is a one-time job and so I would encourage you to spend the time to create a good template.

Here is a tool to create a good Technical Skills template.

1. How exactly is the work accomplished?

- What technical skills must be hired and what can they learn on the job? Usually things that need certifications, degrees and so on must be hired. So also skills, proficiency in which must be proven by the person having worked on a particular project or in a particular organization.

2. What does it take to meet / exceed the objectives of the job?

- What is your measurement to see if performance is excellent? For a person to excel what must they know and be able to do in addition to the basic skills? What kind of previous work experience will be useful for them to have which they can bring to bear on your project right away? Remember: Driver or mechanic?

3. What skills or abilities distinguish the outstanding performer?

- Do you have an environment for sustaining such an employee? What are your plans to create such an environment? How realistic are these plans? To what extent are all the elements involved, in your control?

4. What results can the candidate expect from the job?

- What do his peers get? What is the industry norm? What is the compensation package? What are the career prospects? What are the other intangible benefits of working with you; for example, your company's name may be a 'benefit' on his resume. But then beware that if this is the chief 'benefit' for him, then you will most probably be used as a stepping stone to other places.

Sometimes it is cheaper to hire a skill and at others, especially if you have strong in-house skill training courses, it is cheaper to train the individual after hiring them. The other consideration is time: do you have the time to train or is the need so immediate that you must necessarily hire a 'ready-made' candidate.

Thinking from the perspective of the candidate, you need to be able to explain the following:

Compensation
- The whole package and its tax implications. Also any elements of the perquisites that you believe the candidate must take note of, e.g. any higher education schemes, any globally benchmarked internal training programs (GE's Corporate

University at Crotonville; Motorola's Leadership College etc.).

The nature of work

- Especially any challenges in location or people. You need to be very specific, clear and honest about these. It is a good idea where feasible and especially when recruiting middle and senior management positions to let the candidate spend a few days on-site to get a feel for the place. This will give them an idea of what they are likely to face and for someone with the right attitude, it can be very inspiring in terms of the challenges it presents. It also gives those he is going to work with, an idea of who they will deal with, no matter how brief and is a very useful icebreaker.

When I was recruited to turn around a very troublesome organization with a communist labor union and a totally unionized workforce, I asked to visit the location and spend a week there before I accepted. What I saw there was that in addition to the union issues, the managerial/supervisory staff was totally demoralized; the union literally ran the place and called all the shots. It was this challenge that sold the place to me and I accepted. In two years I built the best team I ever had and we turned the place around and re-created our relationship with the union in such a way that we exceeded all our targets and when I left, the union gave me a farewell citation and gifts.

Prospects for advancement

- Be clear about the rules for promotion in your organization, both the official and 'unofficial' ones. Remember, it is better to risk a high achiever not joining by being truthful and saying, 'We are a family business and have a seniority based advancement policy and there is a glass ceiling above which non-family people can't go', than to say, 'Even though we are a family business, there is no preference for family members and promotions are strictly based on performance,' and then have him find out that you lied through your teeth.

Disillusionment is never restricted to that person alone. It spreads and creates cynicism in the system which will prove very expensive in the long run. So honesty and truthfulness is the best policy. Let the person who joins be clear about why he is joining and what it will take to have a good career. Let him see the other benefits of the job which may well outweigh career advancement in terms of job designations. It is not for nothing that family businesses as a whole have very low attrition and many senior executives prefer the more 'personal' atmosphere of a family business to the cold steel and glass of multinational corporations.

Visibility

- Visibility is major consideration especially in large multinationals in terms of career advancement. Many ambitious people prefer high visibility jobs to better paying ones but which have low visibility. It is important for you as the hiring manager to be clear about what is important to the one you are hiring. In this context, especially if you are hiring for positions which have low visibility – support and service for example – to talk about any job rotation schemes that you have where a person will be rotated to a higher visibility job after some time.

Please be sure that such a scheme is in existence first though, before you promise it to anyone. Also talk to them about other ways of gaining visibility through publishing, speaking at seminars and conferences, internal organizational thought-share and the company intranet.

Location

- It is a good idea to let people see where they will live if they join especially if it is a place with some local peculiarities of a place where the candidate has never been. It is a good idea to send the candidate who makes it to the final selection interview to see the place and spend a few days there, with his spouse, so that he/she can get a feel for the place. Don't assume that a person will like or dislike a place just because of what you think about it.

I was sent to see the place of my first job in Guyana, South America, which was a mining village on the bank of Rio Berbice, 200 miles inside the Amazonian rain forest and I loved it and remained there for 5 years. When I left, it had nothing to do with the job, location or company. So be very open, frank and clear about all the elements of the nature of work and let people form their own opinions, instead of trying to convince them.

Training and development

- What opportunities will be available in this job? More and more today many people especially in their initial years join organizations with a clear goal to gain specific experience. So your organization's reputation in the market for the kind of high-end technology you work on, the global training programs you have, your corporate university, your global presence and the opportunity to work on projects in different countries will all be seen as unique 'selling' points for the job. So talk about them.

But once again a word of caution; being ambitious while painting a picture of your organization in your desire to hire the best is one thing; indulging in fantasy is something else.

Many excellent candidates get very quickly frustrated because they were given a wrong picture by a well meaning over enthusiastic hiring manager which they discover was far from the reality. By all means, speak well of the company and the kind of work you are hiring for but beware of gilding the lily.

 A good friend who was the head of HR for a major American multinational was hired by a large family concern in India with the promise that he would spearhead and oversee the creation of a Corporate University on the lines of the corporate university in his old company. He was very keen to be able to head such an initiative as it would have been a once in a lifetime opportunity. He asked for my opinion. I said to him, 'If you think you will still be able to find fulfilment in the job if nothing comes of the university, take it. Not otherwise.' He disregarded my advice and took the job and lasted six months. He left when he realised that the university promise had been a lure.

The family concern wanted him to help them to become more process driven but were anxious that he wouldn't join only for that reason. So to 'sweeten' the deal they spoke about wanting to create a Corporate University. While this may well have been a desire but it was certainly not on the cards in the near future. If they had been upfront and made this clear, the man may still have stayed on and they would all have benefited.

But the way they did it, he got the feeling that the whole Corporate University thing was only a story without any substance to it and that destroyed their credibility in his eyes and he left. Rather a silly thing to do on the part of the recruiter but then people do silly things.

It is important to let people get pleasant surprises, not nasty shocks.

The Quality Factors Template

The key to creating a good Quality Factors Template is to have total clarity on the Core Values of the company. This seems like stating the obvious but it is surprising how often hiring managers only have the vaguest of ideas about what a particular value means. The problem lies in the fact that most organizations have nice sounding Core Values and Vision Statements but have not done the essential work of creating **'Operative Definitions'** for each value.

An Operative Definition is a statement of observable behavior that will tell you that the particular value is being practiced. Values and attitudes are in the mind or heart of the individual. We can't see them. What we can see and measure are the behaviors that emanate from those values. So it is essential to be clear about the behaviors that will tell you that the value actually exists.

For example, many organizations say that their Core Value is 'Integrity'. But when you are hiring (and indeed in your day to day operations as well) you need to know what work related behavior will tell you that 'Integrity' exists.

What is a person expected to do and not do in order to be working with 'Integrity'? In some companies, integrity may mean honesty with regard to financial dealings. In others it may include standing up for one's rights in the face of opposition. In some others it may mean taking the unpopular stance in the interest of supporting diversity or in the interest of affirmative action. Integrity as indeed almost any other value can have many meanings. But for each of them you need to specify some behaviors that can be observed that will tell you that it is in practice.

To be able to create a good Values Template it is essential to be clear about the values that you want to hire. What do they specifically mean in your organization and what behaviors will tell you that they exist. Some examples below of the most commonly stated values in most organizations will illustrate further what I mean.

Sample Values Template

For each one of these Values (Quality Factors) there must be a clear Operative Definition which describes the behaviors that you would look for to show if the value is being practiced. Only if you are clear can you design your interview questions to probe for them. Take for example 'Integrity'. I have seen organizations where integrity is an absolute value. You either have it or not. It's like being pregnant; either you are or you are not.

You can't be slightly pregnant. So also with integrity. There are no grey areas, no interpretations of integrity.

On the other hand in one of my Core Ideology Workshops, a senior top management/promoter group defined integrity as, 'We will give money (bribes) if necessary but will not give alcohol or provide women.' Believe it or not, I was more shocked than you may be, reading this but I am witness to this. Naturally as a facilitator it was not my role to influence them. But that was the last job I did for them. It is one of my Core Values that I only work with organizations which resonate with my own values.

However the reason I mention this is because 'Integrity' is one of the stated values of that organization. So what do you think will happen to someone who comes in with a different understanding of what integrity means? Clarity about Operative Definitions is essential to hiring right. What must be remembered is that the Skills Template and the Values Template are independent dimensions. A Winner is one who measures up completely on the values and to some extent on skills.

However I would like to emphasize that while some or more of the skills can be taught on the job and may indeed have to be learned there, values must almost always be hired. Values take years of conditioning to inculcate and are mostly the result of upbringing and culture. That is why in the old days, people consciously looked for young people from good families and did reference checks very seriously. This was not about any 'caste system' but about the fact that upbringing is a factor of the family's culture and values. People who come from good families who live by high standards of decency, morality and integrity, bring them into the organization and so it was considered important to look for such people from such families.

Hiring people with the wrong values is extremely expensive, especially in terms of the huge negative effect it can have on the organization's culture and on other people with whom this individual works. Needless to say, in leadership positions, this can be dramatically disastrous. So time spent in creating a well thought-out Values Template is well worth the effort. Reference checks are a very important aid to ensure that you are hiring right. There is no need to be hesitant about them.

Equally important is to design the probing questions that you are going to ask in order to elicit information about whether or not each one of the values you are looking for, actually exists and is practiced. Without this information the interviewer will remain clueless without actual hard data to support his/her assessment.

More about the questions later.

The Interview Guide

A step by step guide to each stage

The Hiring Interview

A conversation with a purpose

Preparation

It is impossible to overemphasize the importance of preparation. It is often the most neglected phase of the interview but potentially the most useful. Time spent in preparation is time well spent. How often have I seen line managers walk into an interview and pick up a CV and that was the first time they'd ever seen it? Some line managers sound very surprised when I talk about the importance of preparing for an interview. They believe that preparing for interviews is the job of the HR person. In fact, preparing for an interview is the job of anyone who is intending to take an interview no matter where in the organization they come from. The better prepared you are, the more effective you will be. Considering that a lot of the organization's time, money and dreams are linked to the effectiveness with which you interview, I think it is only reasonable to expect that you will make the effort to prepare for it. Here are some steps that are essential for you to take to ensure that you make the best of the opportunity.

Review the Operative Definitions of your Values

- The clearer you are about the Operative Definitions, the more likely you are to identify a match.

Remember that the Operative Definition is the behavior/s that defines the value that you are going to probe for. Without clarity about what behaviors to look for you will simply have to go by the candidate's word that he or she actually believes in that value and practices it. This is not good enough. You need hard data but you can't probe unless your Operative Definitions are clear. Remember that you can't create Operative Definitions on the hoof as it were, in the interview room. The Operative Definition of each Value/Quality Factor must be created as a collective exercise of all the Top Management of the organization and cascaded down through the ranks to understand that there is uniform understanding and agreement on each definition. Then these Operative Definitions must form part of the Performance Management/Employee Satisfaction & Customer Service Quality measurement systems.

- So a considerable amount of work has to be done on the Operative Definitions before you can actually use them in your interview. So do remind HR about this.

Once you have the Operative Definitions, I do strongly recommend that you read them before you go into the interview, no matter how well you think you know them. Then again read those before you ask the questions related to each.

For each of the Operative Definitions you need to prepare a set of open ended probing questions to ascertain if the candidate actually practices them or not. If the Operative Definitions are used in your Performance Management system as I have suggested above you may like to take some of the questions from there. If not you will need to create your own questions. Here are a couple of examples:

Integrity: Can you give me an example of any incident from your past where you believed you acted with integrity?

Team Leadership: Please tell me about a challenge you faced as a team leader. Please talk about what was most difficult about it and how you solved this difficulty.

Review the resume and highlight the points you need to probe for

- Having a standard form for your resume is a good idea. Many companies have such forms on the internet which a candidate is obliged to fill. A standard form is beneficial for you because it gives you comparable data between applicants and ensures that all the data that is relevant to you is available. In the absence of a standard form you will need to extract the information you need from the many different kinds of resumes you will receive. Clarity about what information you need is naturally essential. Usually your HR department will do this job for you but if you are a startup, short on HR staff then this may become your baby to deal with. Getting relevant information that is comparable is important in helping you to compare applicants.

- Keep the resume with you and write on it or in the margins. Sometimes looking at the resume as the candidate is speaking throws up useful questions that you can ask to probe on particular issues. Dwell on all the transitions and probe for reasons for moving. Any gaps must be filled by asking questions about the reason for the gap and what the individual did during that time. Let not honesty overshadow facts. For example if someone says that they failed as a consultant and so came back into the corporate world, their answer may sound disarmingly honest, but ask the individual what they learnt from the failure and you may find that they learnt nothing. So if you still hire them, you will be hiring a loser. A nice loser perhaps, but a loser nevertheless.

Review the paperwork

- If the candidate completed any tests or forms, please ensure that you read them before you enter the interview room and make some notes on points that the test or form highlighted. These may be areas to probe and simply skimming through the form as the candidate is sitting across the table is a waste of their and your time. Potentially useful information will be lost and the candidate's time in filling out the form, wasted. Some people like to say that they want to interview the candidate without 'prejudice' and then

look at the information.
This is a big mistake.
There is no prejudice in
having access to good
information. Good information enables you to ask good questions. And once the candidate has left it becomes impractical to ask any questions that may arise when you do look at the tests. Finally let's face it, how many of us have the time or inclination to wade through forms after interviews are over, with only a vague recollection of even who the candidates were? In my view it is important to know as much as possible about the individual before you go into the interview. This will give you ideas about the areas you need to probe. All such pointers are most welcome and you need them. They can save you much time and headache.

Plan your time

Keep a watch and look at it. Especially if you are doing multiple interviews it is very easy to unconsciously allow the time to slip and then start hurrying towards the end of the day. Quality then slips and hiring suffers. So no matter how tedious it may seem to your free spirit, please plan your time and stick to it rigidly. That way you will ensure that you do justice to each candidate and thereby to yourself. For in the end it is primarily for your own benefit that you are doing all this, not for the benefit of the candidates. So it is in your own interest to do it well.

Prepare your Quality Factors Screen

Values	Results orientation	Initiative	Interpersonal skills
Sources			
Work history			
Education			
Self evaluation			69
Interests			

It is critical to be clear in your own mind about what you are looking for. Remember this is often a one-time activity at least in the medium term and so it is worth the effort to do it well and to take the time required. Also if you are not the hiring manager it is essential that you talk to the people who are going to have to live with the people you hire for them and ensure that you have the elements that they need. As I have mentioned earlier, this is not about creating hard-to-get wish lists but to ensure that to the extent possible you have taken into account all the attitudes and behaviors that you and the hiring managers believe as critical to success and which must necessarily be hired. Remember the maxim:

Hire values, Train skills.

You the Interviewer

Take notes

- I can't possibly overemphasize the importance of taking notes. As I mentioned earlier, notes are critical to quality. Especially as you will probably interview more than one person on one day it is entirely likely that you will mix up the data of one with the other and hire the wrong person. Notes are an absolute must for proper interviewing.

- It is important that you alert the candidate about what you are doing because to have someone scribbling while you are talking is very distracting and irritating for the speaker. Also most speakers will stop speaking as soon as you break eye contact to write. So warn the candidate about what you are doing and why. Say to them, 'I would like to ensure that I remember all that you tell me so I am going to take notes as you speak. Please continue to speak and don't let my writing distract you.' This will put them at ease and is the polite thing to do. Smile as you say this, please.

Comprehensive opening statement

- Plan your opening statement to set the stage for mutual candor. Remember that it is only when both you and the candidate are frank and speak freely that you will be able to assess each other correctly and ensure a proper fit. It is a good idea to state this clearly upfront so that the candidate understands that frankness will pay. Continuously reinforce this atmosphere of mutual candor by your behavior and speech.

For example you may begin by saying, "Thank you for coming to see us. In this company we believe that the more we know about each other the better we will be able to decide if we can both achieve our mutual goals. I would like to talk to you about your work history, your education, what you see as your strengths and development areas and what your other interests are. Once we finish with that, I will be happy to answer any questions that you may have about our company and this job. If that is okay with you, would you like to begin by telling me what you enjoyed the most in your last job?"

Open ended questions

- Open ended questions generate information. You need as much as you can get. Sometimes while the candidate is speaking you may realize that either s/he is going into too much detail or that s/he is off on a tangent. A good technique to intervene without causing offence is to call their name.

- Just say, "Sylvia," and you will find that they will stop speaking and look at you. Then you can say something like, "That was very interesting, but could  you tell me about the time you spent on the project to design the security system for the Space Shuttle. What parameters did you consider to be the most critical?"

- You will also find that when you ask a question about the past, the candidate will look up or away or in some cases even shut their eyes momentarily. These are all unconscious behaviors as the brain is doing some data mining from its long term memory. Be aware of that and remain silent. People need that time and if you keep asking more and more questions, which is something that many interviewers do in an attempt to be helpful, you will only confuse them and the delay will be longer. So ask your question once and remain silent and let the person take their time to answer. Then you can ask the next question or probe further depending on what the candidate says. Listen carefully because the answer will give you the cue for further probing.

Facial expression: Neutral & friendly

* Don't be overly effusive or funereal. Be serious but friendly. It is important to be aware that facial expressions are governed by unconscious cultural norms. South Indians for example are mostly very serious and smile only when their life is threatened. Most Indians, especially women, don't smile at strangers. So when they do smile because they are in an interview, it can seem artificial. Similarly there are cultural norms peculiar to Middle Eastern, Japanese, Korean, Malaysian, British and American cultures, which make facial expressions of one the source of much misunderstanding for another. It is good to be aware of what your own cultural default

setting is and make sure that you appear friendly and welcoming.

- Also when interviewing candidates from other cultures it is useful to learn something about their cultures so that you can interpret behavioral queues accurately. Homework always pays. If you have a person from that culture in your organization, you may consider having them on the interview panel to check your own notes with before deciding. The goal is to be as accurate as possible in interpreting data so that your decisions are right.

Posture: Erect, relaxed, still

- Don't make any distracting movements like playing with your pen, doodling on your writing pad and so on. Your posture and movement affects the atmosphere in the room and can vitiate the feeling of trust and openness that you have taken the trouble to create and which you need for a successful interview. There is nothing more distracting and unseemly than a leg that is aspiring to become a pendulum. The value of simply sitting still can't be overemphasized.

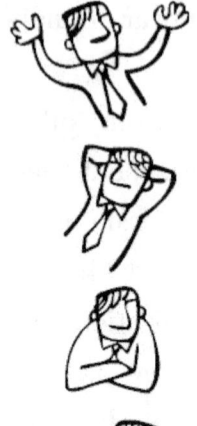 • Sitting with your feet extended towards or pointing towards someone is considered extremely rude in many cultures. Sitting with your feet propped on the table or on a bag of books is considered totally blasphemous and a huge insult to the person sitting across the table from you in all Eastern cultures. Leaning back with your hands behind your neck and your chair tilted back from the floor is seen as very casual and even disrespectful. Shaking hands is another one. Muslim men and women will not shake hands with someone of the opposite gender. Most Indian women are also reluctant to shake hands as in India we prefer to join our hands in a gesture of greeting and respect and don't touch the other person. It is a good thing for the interviewer to be aware of cultural norms so that you don't cause offence or make people uncomfortable.

How you speak: Confident, soft, sensitive

- Remember you are not a police officer and the candidate it not a suspect that you are interrogating. The tone, speed of speech and accent are all important. If you speak with an accent that like blue cheese is an acquired taste, please say right in the beginning, "If you find my accent difficult and I say anything that you don't understand, please ask."

- Speed of speech is also an issue. Most Indians speak fast. Add to this the 'Indian head shake' and you have a situation that only one who is steeped in wisdom can unravel. It is essential to be aware of one's own communication peculiarities and to warn the candidate about what to expect. This kind of frankness breaks the ice and builds mutual trust.

- Many Asians find American accents difficult to deal with and Australian impossible. British Cockney accents and most African accents are equally incomprehensible to outsiders. And of course Indian/Pakistani accents are not the easiest for Europeans and Americans. Add to that some candidates who try to speak in what they consider an American accent because you are American. So patience is of the essence.

 • Another very important thing to remember especially for Indians who are not only multilingual but tend to break into their mother tongues at frequent intervals or to use words from Hindi or Tamil and so on is that this is not acceptable. It is very impolite to speak in a language that your listener can't understand.

• In your speech another important consideration is idiom. Culturally many idioms are not understood in other countries and some are actually offensive. For example, 'Teach an old dog new tricks' can cause offence in India and the Middle East because calling a person a 'dog' is a common curse. Similarly the British old school, 'Go break a leg', which believe it or not is a way of saying 'Farewell, good luck' can be taken literally and look at askance to say the least.

• Most people nowadays don't use terms like, 'Old chap' and other such phrases; but these can seem to be very condescending. Please remember that all our baseball and basket ball phrases (power dunk, hit the ball out of the park) are Greek and Latin for non-Americans. So also is cricket terminology for

Americans. If you do use any of these please take the trouble to explain that a hat trick has nothing to do with hats and a silly mid-on is not a ball that landed by mistake in your lap.

- Tell them that what a 'pitch' is depends on what game you are playing for it is the trajectory of the ball in baseball and mother earth in cricket.

- English is a strange language spoken very differently in various parts of the world with very different accents and idioms; yet it is still called English. So if someone says that they speak English fluently it is not to be assumed that you, Mr. English Speaker will automatically understand them.

- But one thing for sure. If you retain your sense of humor and are willing to ask and answer questions you will have a lot of fun and learn a lot of new ways of expressing yourself in the bargain.

- Finally one last warning about jokes. They are nice to loosen up the person and break the ice but are twice as dangerous as normal speech with respect to their liability to fall flat or cause offence. A joke must be polite and culturally and politically correct. If you are not sure, apply the golden rule – say nothing. Silence is always safe. Just say, 'Hello and welcome.'

 • Cheerfulness is best conveyed with a smile. Very safe, universally understood and universally appreciated. A cheerful demeanor can't be misunderstood and creates an atmosphere of trust.

Political Correctness

- I will talk about questions that are illegal to ask later in more detail but do remember that political correctness is not about insincerity but about showing the respect for people that is in fact their due.

- It is important to know what people of different ethnicity are called in different countries and to use the correct terminology to ensure that you don't cause offence.

- In America a white person is called Caucasian, a black person is African American (not anything else please) and a (Red Indian) is a Native American. To use the term 'Red Indian' is considered highly offensive. 'Asian' in America means Chinese. Indians are from India.

<u>Setting the Stage</u>

<u>Creating a comfortable atmosphere</u>

As I mentioned earlier, it is important to create an atmosphere of trust and make the candidate as comfortable as possible. It is true that some measure of anxiety may still exist but to the extent that it is possible for you, do take the trouble to make the candidate feel comfortable. That way you are more likely to get

 responses that are as close to real-life as possible. Stress interviews create modified behavior and are not useful in helping you to see what a candidate will do in normal circumstances.

It seems redundant to have to say this, but it is essential to ensure that there are no interruptions and distractions during the interview. All phone calls must be diverted, cell phones switched off (not even on silent or meeting modes as they still create distraction) and all visitors banned for the duration of the interview. This is all about respecting the candidate and demonstrating to the candidate what your **operative policy** on treating people is.

It's all very well to say, "We are an organization that respects people and believe in the dignity of the individual....yeda, yeda, yeda, blah, blah, blah..." but then you keep the candidate waiting without explanation or allow interruptions during the interview. Behavior speaks far more loudly and credibly than words and all the spiel about your company's people policy will get the lie if you don't demonstrate respect for the candidate.

 It is good to remember that when you are interviewing, you and your organization are on 'stage' and the candidate will take away an impression irrespective of whether or not, s/he is hired. It should be your endeavor that the **people you don't hire** go away as your Brand Ambassadors and say to the world, "I wish I had been hired because I would love to work for the person who interviewed me." A well conducted interview will have this impact. Beware of talking too much in an attempt to appear friendly. It is your job to get the candidate to talk and to get useful information from him/her.

Not to impress them with your erudite sophistication. If you speak for more than 15% of the time in the interview then you are speaking too much. Many candidates are trained to make you talk by asking questions which tempt you to talk about yourself and your organization and give you a good feeling at the end of it, leading to your hiring the candidate with little useful information about what s/he can do or has done. Later this can become a source of embarrassment for you if the candidate does not work out and you realize that all you needed to do to avoid the mistake was to have spoken less and listened more.

15%

Note taking is absolutely essential to good interviewing. I can't possibly overemphasize this point. Many people have a very high opinion of their retentive memories. The reality is that it is impossible to retain all the data in sequence in your memory alone, especially if you are interviewing multiple candidates as happens in most cases. Data you don't note down will either be lost or will get mixed up and distorted in your mind and lose its integrity.

One of the many benefits of a panel interview is that while one person asks a question and engages the candidate, others can take notes of what the candidate says. That way the candidate can continue to talk to someone who shows interest in what they are saying by being visibly engaged with them, while none of what he or she is saying is lost. Another benefit of a panel interview is the possibility of comparing notes, which is most valuable when assessing multiple candidates for

 the same job. Often it happens that one person may have noted something and arrived at a particular conclusion while another person may either not have seen that behavior at all or may have come to a different conclusion. When the panel members compare notes after the interview it gives them a far richer perspective than if they had interviewed the candidate individually. They will recall incidents and their own reactions and be able to compare notes and so take better decisions than if they had been alone.

The Note Taking Tool

Quality Factors

Name:	Team Leadership	Customer Orientation	Results Orientation	Flexibility Adaptability	Analytical Thinking
Date:					
Work History					
Education					
Self Evaluation					
Interests					

Information Sources

Interview Note Sheet

This tool will help you in taking notes. The tool has **Quality Factors** on the X-axis and **Information Sources** on the Y-axis. For each Information Source you need to go across the Quality Factors row and ask questions which will show you if that Quality Factor is visible in that Information Source. For example in the first Information Source – Work History, you need to ask questions to show if the candidate has demonstrated

Team Leadership, Customer Orientation, Results Orientation, Flexibility/Adaptability and Analytical Thinking in their past.

You may substitute the Quality Factors in the tool with your own organizational values. Please remember to be clear about observable behavior that will tell you that the Quality Factors exists. I have repeated this principle many times simply because it is the single most common and most damaging mistake in interviewing. Apart from not taking notes, of course. Many interviewers tend to get side tracked into detail on one or more factors and do not maintain the rigor of asking all the questions on all the Information Sources. It is the interaction of the Information Sources with the Quality Factors that is the secret of success of this tool. For example the way team leadership is demonstrated during Education is different from how it is seen in a typical work atmosphere. Both are important to give you a comprehensive picture of the individual. Probe for real life examples. People tend to talk about what they aspire to do. Bring them back to what they have done because what they have done is the only sure proof that they can do it again. So probe.

Time Allocation

As I mentioned earlier it is essential to structure the interview and allocate timelines to each stage. And then it is even more essential to stick to them as far as possible. I have suggested some time frames which in my view are adequate to gather sufficient good data on each element. These numbers are indicative and so please feel free to vary them as appropriate. A thumb rule however is to ensure that the maximum time is spent on Work History and some time on each of the others without leaving anything out completely.

One very important thing to remember is that the purpose of the interview is to get as much good information from the candidate as possible. This means that the candidate must speak for the major part of the time. Interviewers who speak for more than 10-15% of the time do so at the cost of the quality of the interview. So please do resist the urge to hold forth at great length. Ask a question and let them answer it. If you feel that you haven't got sufficient data ask them for more. Ask and remain silent to allow them to recollect and tell you. Your job is to ask questions, listen and take notes.

Career Elements	Minutes
■ Introduction	■ 5-10
■ Work history	■ 30-50
■ Education & Training	■ 10-15
■ Self evaluation	■ 5-10
■ Outside interests	■ 10-15
■ Closing	■ as appropriate

Probing for facts

The soul of behavioral interviewing is to probe for facts which will tell you what a person has **actually done.** Without this all you will have to go by will be intentions and wishes and not facts. Asking good questions is therefore, key. Good questions in my experience can't be thought of on the fly as you listen to the candidate speaking. Good questions need to be thought out in advance, practiced with your colleagues to see if they actually give you the information you need and then they need to be written down. This is a one-time exercise, well worth the effort. Do take the time to develop 3-4 questions for each Value that you want to probe for. Once you have these questions written out, you can use what the candidate tells you as a queue to probe further on specific issues.

Here are some examples:

Creativity: Please describe a situation where you used your creativity to solve a problem at work. What was the problem and how did you solve it?

Communication: Please describe what you believe was the toughest communication situation that you have ever dealt with. What was it and what did you do?

Team Building: Please describe a situation where you dealt with team members in situations of conflict. What was the conflict about and what did you do?

Goal Setting: What is the process of goal setting that you follow? Please describe what you do and how you measure achievement of goals.

Assertiveness: Please tell me about a situation where you had to be assertive in giving directions to others. How did you do it?

Energizing: Please tell me about a situation where you were able to energize a flagging team. What was the situation and what did you do?

Analytical Problem Solving: Please tell me about a time when you used any problem solving tool to solve a problem at work. What was the problem? What tool did you use and how did you solve it?

Organization & Planning: Please describe for me how you organize your day and plan your activities. What tools do you use and what is the result?

Leadership: One of the challenges of leadership is to get others to change their behavior. Please give me an example where you were successful in doing this. What was the behavior that you wanted the other person to change? How did you go about it and what was the result? Did you encounter any resistance? How did you overcome it?

Please feel free to develop specific probes pertaining to the quality factors that you are interviewing for. It is an exercise that will pay rich dividends in quality of hiring.

Probes are usually open ended questions. They are an invitation for the candidate to delve deeper and give more detail. They allow the candidate to literally relive their past and tell you what they did in specific situations and why they did that. As I mentioned earlier, please remember to be patient and to allow for behavior like looking away or looking up as people need to do that to collect their thoughts and recollect real life incidents. Please also be patient and remain silent while the candidate thinks. Very often we find that the interviewer gets impatient or anxious and follows up his first question with several other questions, thinking that they are 'clarifying' things for the candidate. Actually this is very distracting and may be totally unnecessary. So unless the silence gets too long, simply remain silent and sit still. If the candidate doesn't understand your question, they will tell you. Then you can clarify.

Be aware of your facial expressions. Smile and look interested. Keep your attention on the candidate. Don't look disinterested, impatient and don't have a 'get-on-with-it-for-god's-sake' expression on your face. Sit still and don't fidget. Most of this stuff is unconscious so you have to remember to be conscious of it.

Open-ended and Closed-ended questions

In an interview you will use both open-ended and closed-ended questions. The purpose of the interview is for you to find out as much as possible about the candidate. Therefore, a key feature of your questions should be to give them a chance to talk. Particularly at the early stages of the interview, you should use open-ended questions.

Open-ended questions are those that can't be answered by a simple 'Yes' or 'No. Typically they need a longer explanation. Asking open-ended questions and listening attentively to the answer also gives you queues about areas you need to probe further. When you see an area you need to probe ask another open-ended question. E.g. 'That is interesting. Can you tell me how exactly you did that?'

'You must be proud of that achievement. What was difficult and what was easy?'

'What was the most difficult aspect of that challenge and how exactly did you overcome it?'

'How did you win the trust of the opposite party in that situation where they were so antagonistic?'

All these and similar questions are open-ended and enable you to learn more and more about the life and experience of the candidate.

Closed-ended questions are those that can be answered by a 'Yes' or 'No' or at best by one or two words. They bring closure to the topic. They 'force' the person to choose. They are more stressful to answer sometimes. They enable you to move from one topic to another.

Open-ended questions keep the conversation going. They open doors to new areas. They provide more and more information. Closed-ended questions force judgment. They present choices to make. They end conversations.

Both types of questions have a place in interviewing. Open-ended to begin with and during the initial stages of the interview and closed-ended when you need to wrap up on one subject and move to another. Asking closed-ended questions too soon can lead to cutting short the interview and closing the door to important information that may have come your way if you had been patient and asked some more open-ended questions. It is fairly easy to rephrase a closed-ended question into an open-ended format. Just takes a little practice.

Closed-Ended Questions	Open-Ended Questions
• Do you like your present job?	• What do you like the most about your present job?
• Is the payroll system you designed being used in your company?	• This new payroll system you designed, tell me more about it.
• Did you have any difficult moments in your last job?	• What is your opinion about people having to work on weekends?
• Did you work on weekends?	• What did you like best about working in America?
• Did you like working in America?	• What did you like about your manager's style?
• Did you get along with your manager in your last job?	• How did you solve conflicts with your team? Please give me some examples from your past.
• Did you have any problems with your team?	

Leading questions

One of the most common mistakes that interviewers make is to telegraph their preferences and give hints about what would be 'acceptable' answers. The candidate will almost certainly oblige by giving you just the answer that you are looking for. Such questions give you no real information and can mislead you about the real values, opinions and experience of the candidate. Another way that leading happens is when you share a lot of information, consciously or unconsciously by your body language, tone of voice and facial expressions about your own personal preferences, likes and dislikes. Alert candidates will pick up all these cues and answer in ways that they think will be more acceptable to you.

It is very important to be neutral and not to telegraph preferences so that you can get some real information about the candidate's own values, ethics, beliefs and behavior. If you are in doubt about a particular question being 'leading', try it on someone else before the interview and you will immediately see the problem.

Examples of Leading Questions:

- You have experience of working with design engineers, haven't you?
- Wouldn't you say that the government is doing a good thing in privatizing public sector companies?

It is a brave, unusually honest or foolish interviewee who doesn't accept and agree with the answer so waiting to be agreed with.

Leading

- You have experience of working with engineers, haven't you?
- Wouldn't you say that the government is doing a good thing in privatizing public sector companies?
- Labor unions are a nuisance and the enemies of productivity aren't they?

Probing

- Can you tell me about your experience working with design engineers?
- What is your opinion about the government's privatization program?
- I see that you have worked in unionized environments. Can you share some learnings about dealing with militant unions?

Some probing questions:

1. "Tell me about how you managed to ...

2. "How did you feel about ...

3. "What led you to ...

4. "How did you go about ...

5. "What made you decide to ...

6. "What satisfaction did you get from...?

7. We all have occasional disagreements with our managers. What is the most significant disagreement that you had and how did you handle it?

8. If you could change two things about yourself, what would they be?

9. What kind of work brings out the best in you and why?

10. In what ways are you different today than you were five years ago?

As you go on, try to develop your own probes depending on the kinds of jobs you hire for. If you have been taking notes, all you need to do is to go back over your notes when you are free and identify which probes got you the best responses. That is why it is a good thing to take notes and to read them later after the interview to see what you can learn from them.

I am aware that I am repeating myself about the importance of taking notes. It is the single most valuable thing to do but the thing that most people fail to do most often. Without notes not only are you most likely to make huge blunders in hiring but you also have no record of what you did well and what you didn't so you have no way of leveraging any of those learnings when you have no record of what you did or what happened.

Soft & Hard Probes

As a general rule it is desirable to keep the probes soft (you can still be specific) and then follow-up with more probes rather than taking the hard approach. That way people are encouraged to keep talking and to taking you into confidence and telling you real facts.

Hard probes create tension and vitiate the atmosphere of safety and comfort that you have done so much to create. They sound rude, can cause offence and are certainly conversation stoppers. That would be counterproductive because you want the candidate to speak and share more information. Remember that you always have the option of taking the harder approach. Only, don't do it unless you have to.

Hard or Direct	Softer and better
• Why did you leave that job?	• What made you look for a change?
• Why do you think you had trouble with your boss?	• What were the areas of difference with your supervisor?
• Why did you switch from engineering to business?	• How did you make the decision to switch from engineering to business? Was it a tough choice?
• Why did you decide to take a pay cut to take that job?	• What were the advantages in the new job that made it worth the pay cut?

Keeping the candidate talking

The important thing is to get the candidate to talk and to share as much useful information as possible about himself and his experience as possible in the time that you have. Expressing disapproval or any negative judgment tends to discourage people from talking, while smiling, nodding and showing approval encourages them to speak. Please remember that the interview is simply a place for you to get information. Not to exchange ideas, argue, socialize, convince or influence the candidate.

- Appear to agree or understand
- Don't show disapproval
- Don't show shock or surprise
- Reinforce / reward verbally and non-verbally
- Play down unfavorable information

 Body language, facial expressions, reinforcement by encouraging sounds or words are all very important in maintaining an atmosphere that is conducive to information sharing. Remember that the candidate's personal achievements may not be very impressive to you today from your own perspective of far greater experience. However it is important not to appear to disregard or run down his/her achievements. It is important to try to put yourself in their place and see what they have done.

Acknowledge that what they did is significant in terms of who they are.

- Say, 'That must have been very satisfying for you. Tell me how you were able to overcome the challenges in this task.'
- Say, 'I must say that is a tremendous achievement for anyone. Tell me how did you plan for this?'
- Say, 'You must be proud of having won this honor. Tell me how you managed your time and other priorities while you studied for these exams?'

Just listen and ask any questions that you need to get good supporting information so that you can decide.

Remember that you are not a psychoanalyst and are not trying to understand the workings of the candidate's mind. All you need to know is what they did in a particular situation as it will tell you what they are most likely to do again.

Active Listening

Paraphrasing or Active Listening is a very good tool to help you to understand the candidate and build trust as well as to probe further to get more information. Paraphrasing consists of sharing your understanding of what the person said with them so that they feel comfortable about having conveyed what they wanted to. So you would say, 'That is interesting. So if I understand you correctly, you are saying that you climbed Mount Everest in your socks. Is that correct?' Then if the person agrees that you understood them correctly, say, 'Thank you, please go on. What happened next?' Do remember that it is not your job to agree or disagree with the candidate. It is your job to understand what they are telling you and to get as much data about it as possible. So you would not say, 'O come on! How can anyone climb Mount Everest in their socks?' You would only note that the candidate said that he did.

Listening Reminder

1. You should not talk more than 15% of the time
2. The person will look away, up or down or even shut their eyes to think
3. They may need some time to recollect data.
4. Don't interrupt with another question because you are getting anxious
5. Smile and look encouraging. Nod, show signs of interest, use encouraging words or sounds
6. Don't telegraph your internal reactions, agreements or disagreements, likes or dislikes

7. Be comfortable with silence

Work History

You can start in this way:

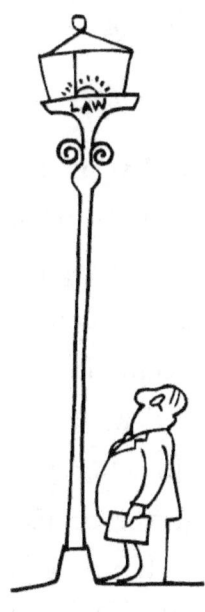

"Would you like to begin by telling me about your work experience, starting with your last job? Tell me about each job, your challenges, your likes and dislikes and any special accomplishments."

It is better to start with the last job because it is most current and of most relevance to you. What they did a decade ago is at best interesting but not much else. What they did most recently is what they are most likely to be able to do for you as well and so that is more relevant to you. It is most important to clearly ascertain what a person actually did; his personal contribution to the task because that is the only thing that you can be certain that they can replicate for you. What they have not done, their dreams and aspirations may sound good but remember that those are all in the realm of hope, intention and desire. Not fact. You may still hire them in order to experiment and give them the opportunity to see what they can accomplish. That is a risk that you are taking and it is essential to be aware of this. I am not discouraging risk taking. I am merely distinguishing between risk taking and guaranteeing results.

By careful probing it is possible to get hard verifiable data about what a person's accomplishments were, what difficulties they had to surmount in order to accomplish their goals. Their strategic vision and planning capability as well as their perseverance and commitment to fulfilling what they started. Their risk taking capability; whether while observing them in action you are likely to feel like a comfortable observer or like someone who is white nailed, screaming in terror on a roller coaster without brakes. This is the classical entrepreneurial profile with legendary brinkmanship, should be strictly left alone to create their own corporations. They always make lousy employees. Unless of course you have the maturity to handle them and the ability to provide them with opportunity.

It is essential to probe to see what a person did himself. It is nice to hear people talking always in an inclusive manner but you need to be sure if you are hiring the leader of the team or the only passenger who had to leave because the team finally got sick of carrying the dead weight. Remember the story of the elephant and the ant riding on his back. When the elephant crossed the bridge, the ant said, 'Wow! When we crossed the bridge it shook.' You need to be sure if you are interviewing the elephant or the ant.

While asking questions therefore, it is very important to dwell on the transitions; reasons for change, what they expected to get from the change, did they actually get it when they made the change, what was their learning and so on. Probe especially for learnings from mistakes. If they learnt something useful from previous mistakes you can be sure that they will not make the same mistakes at your expense. Listen to how they explain the mistake. Do they own responsibility or do they shift it? There is a story about a CEO who would not hire anyone who said that he had never made a mistake in his life. That is a good policy as long as you ensure that you probe for the learnings. There is no value in making mistakes if there is no learning at the end of it. And learning will not happen unless the person has a method of extracting learnings. So ask them about it.

Listen for tones of owning responsibility, blaming, acknowledging the contribution of others to their own success, seeking and giving feedback, analyzing their own performance and evaluating themselves at the end. These are all indicators of attitude which is the one area that you can truly leverage. It is also the one area where if you make a mistake, it will be the most costly.

Key Questions

1. Why was that job taken?
2. Duties and responsibilities?
3. Accomplishments (quantify)?
4. Likes and dislikes?
5. Reasons for changes?
6. Leadership experience?
7. Supervision / independence?
8. Career changes-why?
9. Summarize and move on...

Education

One you have enough information about their work, you can move on to their education.

You may like to say, "Thanks for that. Now tell me about your education. I see that you have an MBA which you did after your engineering. Why did you think of an MBA instead of an MS?"

 While education is important, it is secondary, especially at senior positions where actual work accomplishment is more essential. However good grades are indicative of focus so you may like to ask about grades especially to younger people. You can ask about their choice of subjects, how they leveraged their learning in practice, how they are able to translate theory into practical applications are all areas that can be probed for. With senior people grades are unimportant so you wouldn't ask about them unless it is

to acknowledge some major achievement like a gold medal in university.

In this section you can also ask about extracurricular activity at university which can give you pointers towards leadership qualities or potential areas of conflict. For example if the person was a union leader then it would indicate organizing ability as well as the tendency to challenge policies. If they also had a fellowship and taught it would indicate skill in managing time as well as teaching. If they wrote any books/papers or made presentations at seminars then it would indicate structured thinking, conceptualization and of course presentation. See if they were engaged in any social development, voluntary activity. Much to look for.

Key Questions

1. Best and poorest subjects – why?
2. Grades / rank / scores?
3. Extracurricular activities?
4. Leadership roles?
5. Honors?
6. Work effort?

7. Reason for college / major subject choice?

8. Analytical ability / Innovativeness / Initiative?

9. Summarize and move on...

Self Evaluation

This is an area that is also a sincerity check for the candidate. How a person answers your questions about himself can indicate attitude, values and analytical ability. Answers can also point towards truthfulness, confidence and learning ability.

You may ask:

"Thinking back about the jobs that you had, what do suppose a job must have, to give you satisfaction? What would you say are your major strengths? What would you say is your major development need?"

Some people will try to couch weaknesses to look like strengths. For example a person may be very pushy and may lack interpersonal skills to get people to commit to a project. But instead of telling you that, he says, "I get very impatient with slow work." Since nobody in their right mind wants slow work, you may be impressed with this answer. But then ask, 'What do you do to speed people up when you encounter slow work? Please give me a real life example of such a situation?' The thing to do is to ask for examples of situations where the candidate exhibited this impatience. If you probe enough you will discover the underlying lack of social skills. This is a trainable matter and so is not a disqualifying factor in itself, however the attempt to disguise it as something else is another matter.

Key Questions

1. Structured / Unstructured
2. Hands-on / Conceptual / Change
3. Influence / Power
4. Achievement / Status

Strengths?

Ask, "Looking back, what do you suppose you learned about yourself and your strengths as a result of your work and education experience?"

While listening to them speak about strengths do probe for skills in those areas. Many times people talk about their interests as being their strengths. A strength is something that you have a talent for, abiding interest in,  that you are very good at and have a lot of skill in and in which you can be sure of near perfect results every time you do it. Something that you have an interest in and do sometimes is a hobby, not a strength. What you want is someone who has the skills along with the interest and talent. So probe for that.

So if a person says, 'My strength is interpersonal relations', ask, 'That is a very important area. Can you please tell me some incidents where you faced challenges in interpersonal relations, what was the challenge, what did you do, how was it resolved?' Many people are very skilled in interpersonal relations as a result of having worked in highly labor intensive, unionized workplaces. They may not have read many books about IPR nor may they have a formal university degree in it but they would have enough practical knowledge to teach a university course. So asking about real life experience is the key to knowing if this is so.

Development needs?

Ask, "How about clues to your development needs as a result of your prior experience? In your case what would you say these would be?"

While listening look for sincerity once again. Also for evidence of structured development planning. Can they show you evidence of how they overcame a weakness? How did they diagnose it, how did they plan to overcome it and what exactly did they do and what was the outcome? Look to see if the person actually worked on a development need. Many people like to talk proudly of development needs which remain as such years later. 'I need to learn how to manage my time,' says one. Ask, 'Excellent. So what system are you following and how successful have you been? Please give me examples.'

Other Interests

Extracurricular activities indicate social responsibility, temperament, what factors may create stress for the individual, sociability and so on.

Key Questions

1. What do you do other than work and why is that interesting to you?
2. Where do you see yourself 5 years from now in terms of your career?
3. How important is that to you?
4. What are you doing today that will ensure that you will achieve your ambition?
5. Why is it important for you to do this kind of work?
6. What books did you read in the last three months and why did you choose those?

Follow-up Questions

This is where note taking will be most useful because it will help you to retain data about what the candidate said earlier in order to probe further. With good notes, you can get the candidate to talk more on something where you need more confirmation. You can probe for more depth to get at the details of what they did in their previous jobs. You can ask for clarifications and test any hypothesis or assumptions that you may have made during the conversation. It is essential to test and confirm all assumptions or you may come to the wrong conclusions and lose a good candidate or worse still, hire a loser.

Follow-up questions give you the opportunity to close any loops and to tie up the loose ends. Some thoughts that you may want to keep in mind:

- Reminders
- Clarification
- Probe for more depth
- Test hypotheses
- Control

Closing

Once you have all the information you need, you can start to bring the interview to a close.

- Ask for and answer questions
- Make your sales pitch: But be real
- Close: Say what happens next
- Follow-up as required

Answer any questions that the candidate may have about your company or the job. If you think there is something that they need to know but which they have not asked, prompt them to ask.

For example, "You have not asked me about transfers and working in all our locations." This is important to enable the candidate to make an informed choice about your organization.

While it is understandable and even desirable that you speak about your company in glowing terms, please beware of mythologizing it. Make sure that what you say is factually correct. I have seen too many instances of people being very disappointed after being hired because the reality was so different from the picture painted for them in the interview. This is a very demoralizing thing. Beware of making promises you cannot keep. It is important to be frank and clear about the information you give about the job and company. But don't over or understate the reality or create imaginary scenarios in your anxiety to appear attractive as an employer. Say it like it is. It is better for the

candidate to be delightfully surprised than to be horribly shocked when they face the actual reality of work.

Please tell the candidate what the next steps are after this interview. Will there be more interviews? If so how many and with whom? How long will the decision making process take? If they are selected how much time will they have to join? Be sure here not to imply that they have been selected already. If you are not clear it can lead to embarrassing and even expensive misunderstandings. You may need to clarify some of these with your HR Head first. It is important that any time lines you mentioned are adhered to or at the very least; you call the candidate and warn them in advance of any impending delays. It is important to remember that the responsibility for the candidate is not over when the interview is over, but remains yours until the whole transaction is settled. It is in these follow-up issues that many organizations lose the opportunity to create brand ambassadors for themselves and instead create people who do not speak well of them because of the way they were treated after the interview.

Please remember that the candidate is most likely to be anxious for news and if you leave him high and dry for too long he will either lose interest or go somewhere else. So if you are seriously interested in a candidate it is essential that you follow up with your organization to ensure that all follow up work is being done in a timely manner and that the candidate has not been abandoned to his own devices.

The MOST HOLY Law – Take notes:

Take notes: Please remember that good note taking is absolutely essential to a good interview. If you don't take notes, you can rest assured that you will make a bad choice. Notes taking may seem tedious but without notes you are sunk. So please do take the trouble seriously.

About good note taking

Note taking is absolutely essential to doing a good interview. Without good notes, you can never be sure of the data that you spent all this time in gathering and naturally the decision at the end will have a high chance of being wrong. So what are 'Good Notes'?

There are some rules for good note taking:

1. Write their words, not your interpretation
2. Write your questions, especially any follow-up questions
3. Write any new things they say, especially if they change what they said first
4. Let them see that you are writing and what you are writing

Be sure to write your questions also in the notes or occasionally the notes may not make sense. If the candidate asked a question and you answered, be sure to record his/her question as well. There is no such thing as 'too many notes'; so feel free to write as much as you want. You may experiment with a recording device but ensure you take permission to use it as there may be legal implications. I find plain and simple pen and paper the best and most versatile and easiest to recall.

Evaluating the Candidate

Once you have all the data you need, close the interview and send the candidate away. Then try to do the analysis as soon thereafter as possible while the information is still fresh in your mind. Your notes will be the most helpful tool that you have but even with good notes, sometimes if too much time passes between an interview and its evaluation, the mind plays games.

Some common interview traps are as follows:

1. **Selective attention**
   a. Hearing only what fits your hypothesis. Undervaluing positive info; over sensitive to negative. Getting distracted during the interview and losing information.

2. **Selective judgment**
   a. Not using all information. Making decisions early in interview and then closing your mind to contrary information. This is a very common fault.

3. **Halo Affect**
    a. Basing evaluation on only a few facts. Undifferentiated judgment
4. **Contrast Effect**
    a. Letting overall evaluation, mask profile of strengths and weaknesses
5. **Influence of Misleading Signs**
    a. Judgment is influenced by other candidates- appearance, glibness, and similarity to self or model employee.

Legal Issues

It is important to be knowledgeable about legislation that may apply to recruitment in the country that you are recruiting in. I have mentioned below special issues related to recruiting in the United States of America. But similar laws may apply in other countries as well. Legal mistakes can be very painful and expensive and may end up costing you your job. So take expert advice. That is cheaper than paying the cost of litigation later. Remember it is more important to know what not to say.

What is legal and what is not?

Technically, it is illegal for an interviewer to ask anything personal that is not directly job-related. Off-limit questions include (but are not limited to): information regarding age, marital status, and country of origin, religion, sexual preference and health status. Almost any legal information about the candidate may be illegal in the job interview.

There are some exceptions to this rule however. Personal questions that are clearly job-related are usually allowed in the interview or on the job application. If you have any doubts please consult your legal counsel.

Legal Personal Questions:

1. Have you ever been convicted of a crime?
2. What is your status with regard to a work permit to work in this country?
3. Can you perform the job's essential functions with or without reasonable accommodation? (This

question must be accompanied by a job description covering the essential functions.)

Illegal Personal Questions:

1. Are you married?
2. Do you have children? How many?
3. Do you have any disabilities?
4. How old are you?
5. What is your religion?

Any personal question that does not immediately concern the job is illegal. Play safe. It can be expensive.

The 3 Big Ones

There are three important laws that govern recruitment in the United States. I have described them briefly in terms of what they intend to achieve. This is not a legal explanation and does not constitute a legal opinion. You are advised to consult an attorney who specializes in this branch of law to fully understand all their implications. Please also ensure that you run a short course for all your interviewers so that they don't run afoul of the law. Never go into an interview without knowing the law.

Equal Employment Opportunity (EEO) Act:

This law guarantees the employee the right to be hired without prejudice to his or her gender, race, religion, age, appearance or any other matter. Any questions that you ask which may be seen as probing into these prohibited areas are likely to seen as objectionable. It is for this reason that psychometric testing is illegal for hiring and instruments like the MBTI and others are not used for hiring. Quite apart from the fact of course that psychometric tests during hiring always give wrong results as people are under stress.

While teaching 'Hiring Winners' in the United States, I have heard many real life stories from participants who got themselves into trouble because they asked the wrong question even though their intention was not to discriminate. Many people ask things in an attempt to be friendly and to put the candidate at ease. Unfortunately these questions can become the basis of complaints alleging violation of EEO law. Nothing will happen if you hire the person. But if you don't hire them for your own legitimate reasons, they can allege that you rejected them because of information you got from them illegally.

I remember one incident where a participant in my course, who came from one of the largest multinationals in the telecom sector, reported as follows:

"I interviewed a young woman for a secretarial job. At the end of the interview I told her that we would get back to her about her selection. That evening I was in a shopping mall and saw this young woman with a baby in a pram. I recognized her and said to her, "Hi! Lovely to see you again. Is this your baby? What a lovely baby!! He must be quite a handful, no?" After some more such small talk we parted company.

The following week when the interview results came in, this lady was not hired as she did not meet some of our essential requirements. However when she received the letter, the young lady sued us for discrimination saying that because I had seen her baby in the mall I assumed that she would not be able to work and so had not selected her. We eventually settled out of court with her attorneys."

Seemingly harmless comments can get you into trouble if you are not aware of the laws that govern hiring.

Sexual Harassment Act:

This law guarantees the employee an environment that is free from sexual harassment. Remember that the one who decides what is sexual harassment is the candidate, not you. So please refrain from any jokes, innuendos, remarks or indicators which are likely to be interpreted as being of a sexual nature. It may seem strange to you when you read the Sexual Harassment Act that a society that is as permissive as the USA can have an act that is so strictly puritanical. But the intention is to ensure that the workplace is free from anything that may be offensive to anyone. This extends to the interview as well. Commenting on the personal appearance of the candidate is a commonly committed mistake.

Americans with Disabilities (ADA) Act:

This law guarantees the employee the opportunity to be employed without his / her physical impairment becoming a hindrance except in cases where it may prove to be a hazard for himself or others. In such cases, the onus of proving the hazardous nature of the proposed position is on you.

In all these laws, the onus of proof is on the accused. The employer is bound to conduct an enquiry as soon as they receive a complaint about a possible breach and to publish this report to the competent authority.

Liability is both singular and joint, with the individual interviewer and his company being liable for further action. The investigation itself is often worse than the punishment.

For example if you are accused of sexual harassment, then the investigators will talk to all those who know you, including your family, friends, neighbors, colleagues and so on and ask them if you ever did or said anything that had some sexual connotation which could have been seen as sexual harassment. Imagine what such an investigation is likely to do to the reputation of the individual even if at the end everyone answers with an emphatic denial. There have been incidents of people changing their jobs and location after being proved innocent.

In this context also **please try not to use humor** unless you are sure about what you are saying. I have a fund of stories especially from the US where interviewers got themselves into serious difficulties by simply trying to be funny, chatty or overly friendly. As I say to people who come to my course, **'Hiring Winners'**....... "You don't have to like the law. You only need to know that it is the law and to respect it."

If you have a doubt about what laws apply and what kinds of questions are illegal to ask, please check with you Legal Department. It is a good idea for all hiring managers to do a course on employment laws as applicable to the country.

Ready Reckoner

A quick recall tool to ensure that you are doing everything right.

Pre-Interview

1. Have you gone over your Skills Template and your Values Template once again to make sure that you have made any necessary changes?

2. Are your opening questions clear in your mind? Have you noted them down?

3. Are you clear what you must hire and what you can train?

4. Are you clear what you must probe for?

5. Have you seen the CV of the person you are going to interview so that it is clear in your mind?

Logistics

1. Have you arranged for the place and no interruptions?

2. Have you confirmed the time of the interview to make sure that you are there a little before the candidate arrives?

3. Have you arranged for the candidate to be shown to the room where you will be and without any confusion?

4. Is there provision for tea, coffee, water to be served if needed?

5. Is the seating comfortable and un-intimidating?

Interview Itself

1. Are you using the Interview Tool provided in this book?

2. Have you planned your time and are you following your timetable?

3. Are you taking notes? Are you taking notes? Are you taking notes?

4. Are you aware of yourself and your own prejudices, stereotypes?

5. Are you probing enough to get to real data?

Post Interview

1. Did you invite and answer all the candidate's questions?

2. Did you make any promises? Can you deliver on them?
3. Did you tell them what happens next?
4. Did you thank them for coming?
5. Did you smile and see them off?

Conclusion

Interviewing is the single most powerful process for creating and influencing organization climate and culture. It is important to do it with the care that it deserves. Because its effects last a long time.

Please remember that interviewing is not only about hiring. It is also about brand building and is one of the most cost effective ways of doing this.

At the end of the interview the people you **<u>did not hire</u>** should leave with a longing to work for you. If that happens you can rest assured that a lot of goodwill about the company will spread in the market.

After all, image is everything.

Mirza Yawar Baig

Founder & President of YAWAR BAIG & ASSOCIATES™, International Speaker, Coach, Trainer, Author and Facilitator specializing in helping people become leaders in all aspects of life. His book, **'The Business of Family Business'** shows family businesses how to transform from being 'Person-driven to becoming Process-driven'. Yawar works as a life coach and mentor for prominent business families in India, South Africa & Sri Lanka. He transcends cultural boundaries by blending Eastern values with Western systems. His latest book, **'An Entrepreneur's Diary'** traces his own journey as an entrepreneur and shows how to translate theory into practice that pays. Yawar's style comprises openness, commitment to quality and value-based professionalism. Yawar speaks five languages.

Yawar successfully trained more than 200,000 managers, teachers, business leaders, clergy, politicians, technologists, military and police officers, administrators and students in America, Africa and Asia for over 27 years and developed a reputation for communicating effectively across boundaries of culture, function and nationality. His interventions based on the application of Leadership & Management fundamentals in an experiential learning format, and aided by processes to monitor knowledge retention and skill application are aimed at identifying leadership potential and nurturing it. Yawar works with Leaders at all levels in government and industry, to reduce the negative impact of change on the people while moving toward process improvement.

www.yawarbaig.com   yawarbaig@gmail.com

212

www.ingramcontent.com/pod-product-compliance
Lightning Source LLC
Chambersburg PA
CBHW071420170526
45165CB00001B/339